Dogfight Days

The glorious achievement of Lieutenant Warneford, V.C.

Dogfight Days
British Airmen in Combat
During the First World War

Eric Wood

Dogfight Days
British Airmen in Combat During the First World War
by Eric Wood

First published under the title
Thrilling Deeds of British Airmen

Leonaur is an imprint of Oakpast Ltd
Copyright in this form © 2012 Oakpast Ltd

ISBN: 978-0-85706-904-7 (hardcover)
ISBN: 978-0-85706-905-4 (softcover)

http://www.leonaur.com

Publisher's Notes

The views expressed in this book are not necessarily those of the publisher.

Contents

Preface	7
'The Spotters'	9
Some Stories of 'Rupert'	15
Some Fine British Raids	21
The Pluck of Major Brabazon Rees	32
The End of the "Königsberg"	38
"One of Our Machines Did Not Return"	44
First-Aid in Midair	54
Warneford, V.C.	58
Flying While Dying	63
Rescued by Airmen	67
Tales of the Coast Patrol	73
A Batch of V.C.s	85
The Man who Brought Down Immelmann	95
Some Zeppelin Strafers	102
On Fire!	118
The Battle of Seventy Aeroplanes	121
On Patrol	126
Against Great Odds	132

Some Anonymous Heroes	135
The Train Bombers	143
A Champion Aerial Fighter	149

Preface

In this war of wonders to many people the most wonderful thing is, perhaps, the part which aircraft has played. Very few of us realized less than three years ago what a formidable weapon aircraft was to prove, and most of us can remember the days—they seem not so very distant—when flying was treated as a great mad joke save on occasion when it became a tragedy through some 'mad-brained enthusiast' being killed during an experimental flight. Novelists, who are free to be prophets, naturally seized upon the subject of flight and predicted all sorts of things which perhaps they themselves did not believe would happen; a few men, wiser than their generation, and gifted with far-seeing eyes, seriously insisted on the military importance of aircraft in the near future, but people generally believed that many years must elapse before aircraft could be of practical value. Then came the war, which in due course revealed unsuspected uses to which aircraft could be put.

Very soon it was discovered that the flying men were the eyes of the navies and of the armies, and as time went on it was realized that the side which obtained ascendancy in the air was well on the way to victory. It is now safe to predict, in view of all that has happened, that aircraft will play a decisive part in the final stages of the mighty conflict. The increased range of the heaviest guns, both naval and military, demand methods of observation different from any previously known and utilized; in fact, it may be said that long-range guns—at least guns of such a range as now in use—have been made effectively possible only by aerial observation. The character of trench warfare, also, similar in some respects to, yet in others very different from, the war of trenches in other conflicts, has demanded the aerial scout, even as that latest ingenious war device, the tank, calls for assistance from the aeroplane.

This little book, however, is not a serious study of aircraft in war, but, as its title indicates, a compilation of thrilling deeds of British airmen chosen from a very large number to illustrate various types and phases of aerial operations. Sometimes the telling has been in the nature of making bricks without straw, because of the absence of details in so many official reports. I trust, however, that in expanding such terse accounts of what obviously were heroic incidents I have not done violence to truth. My aim has been to present what were probably the facts, and I have carefully followed the suggestions contained in the brief originals with that object in view. What wonderful stories, indeed, must be hidden behind some of the cold phraseology of official *communiqués*! What courage, what sheer audacity! Someday, perhaps, we may be allowed to know more, and then the world will be thrilled indeed.

I am aware that many of our gallant flying men desire to remain anonymous, and because of that the only cases in which names are given in the book are those in which the official reports have lifted the curtain of anonymity. Very often details could have been given which would have made certain things much clearer, but discretion demanded that those details should be omitted, as being in the nature of secrets.

The book is intended to be a tribute to the gallant men of the air—the humble tribute of one who is not a flier, but who has a great admiration for those who are. I hope that it may be privileged to play some small part in keeping alive the widespread interest which has been aroused in the doings of the Flying Services.

E. W.

CHAPTER 1

'The Spotters'

In the changed conditions of modern warfare airmen have become the eyes of the army. Starting from their bases, aviators wing their way over the enemy's lines and observe every passing thing that comes within their vision, so that generals, sitting at headquarters, know exactly to where enemy reinforcements have gone, how many trains of munitions have been sent to certain places, where batteries are placed, and a thousand things that the brains of an army must be cognizant of. Trenches dug overnight are noted the next morning and inscribed upon the large-scale maps which are used as bases for the plans of operations. In fact, little that happens escapes notice—if the flying corps of an army has won command of the air.

In yet another sense are airmen the eyes of an army. During a bombardment observers, hovering over the field of battle, note the effect of artillery fire, obtain the range and wireless it back to the batteries; then, when the guns have hurled forth their bolts of destruction, they observe whether the range is accurate, and, if not, signal back instant correction. So the work goes on—and always under intense fire from anti-aircraft guns, for the enemy knows how vital to the batteries hidden away back behind the front lines is the 'spotting' of the aerial onlookers. It is work to try the strongest nerves, for the aeroplane is continually dodging like some giant dragon-fly, in the effort to avoid screaming shells, bursting shrapnel, or some enemy machine that has been sent up to put an end to the work of observation. Quick calculations have to be made, and made accurately, otherwise shells, each costing hundreds of pounds, may be flung across No Man's Land only to tear up vacant fields. Failure to explode in some vital place will cost many valuable lives when the infantry advance.

The following stories illustrate the peril and the glory involved in the work of 'spotting' on active service.

It naturally follows that when aeroplanes are on artillery observation service, enemy 'planes, as we have indicated, endeavour to bring them down or else to drive them away, and such efforts lead to aerial combats. During a battle on July 6, 1915, one of our 'spotting' machines was strenuously attacked by German aviators, after it had been found hopeless to try to drive it away by gunfire. In those days the 'spotters' had to be fighters too, because aerial tactics had not developed into such a fine art as it is today, when the observing machines are protected by fighting 'planes which fly much higher to keep a lookout for and to attack any enemy machines which may attempt to engage the 'spotters.'

The British artillery was doing good work, thanks to the information from the officers flying in the British machine. These were the pilot, Second-Lieutenant Dwight Filley, R.F.C. (Special Reserve), and Lieutenant Lambert Playfair (1st Royal Scots and R.F.C), who was acting as observer. Their 'spotting' had resulted in so many direct hits that, the hostile anti-aircraft guns having proved ineffectual, a number of German fighting machines were sent up to attack them. As one by one they rose to the attack the gallant pilot of the British machine, with a word through the speaking-tube to his observer, made a drive which brought him alongside or above the enemy, and a fair supply of ammunition for the machine-gun being to hand, it was expended to such good purpose that one after another the Germans were compelled to retire. In the breathing spaces between the different combats Filley would drop back into position favourable for observation, and Playfair would resume his interrupted work of taking notes and sending back news to the battery.

The work in hand was important enough to call for all the attention of the two officers, but so far as they themselves were concerned, they did not seem to mind the interruptions. Down below, however, the Germans were becoming greatly exasperated, and finally some officer, having apparently made up his mind that the British aeroplane must be brought down or driven off if the position were to be tenable much longer, sent up a couple of aeroplanes simultaneously, with instructions to attack together.

One can, in imagination, hear one of the British airmen shouting through the speaking-tube: "Now for it!" or see the other passing to his companion a slip of paper with a few words scribbled upon it telling him to get ready for the scrap, with the added titbit: "There are only five rounds left!"

A final message was sent back to the battery, and then, while a shell from one of the guns crashed on to the spot indicated, Filley, without waiting for the Germans to attack him, swooped toward them in order to get in the first shots. It was a right royal battle while it lasted, but, unfortunately, it did not last very long. The British were badly outmatched, being short of ammunition and having two enemies to fight. Filley, however, manoeuvred his machine so skilfully, and Playfair worked his gun so cleverly, that, but for an unlucky bullet from one of the German machines, they might have come off with flying colours. That bullet, however, put an end to Filley's hopes, for Lieutenant Playfair was killed in the very act of firing his gun.

Practised as he was in the ways of engines, Lieutenant Filley, after recovering from the shock he had suffered at seeing his comrade killed, realized that his engine had been damaged by some of the spraying bullets from the German gun. He was helpless for attack now that his companion was dead, and his one idea henceforth was to save his machine. To stay where he was would mean being shot down by the Germans, in which case the aeroplane would be captured and he himself made prisoner, even if he were not killed.

The true soldier knows when it is time to leave the scene of battle, and Filley realized that his duty was to get back as quickly as possible. The enemy, thinking that they now had him, closed in upon him, but the Lieutenant swung round, and, with his engine making weird noises, as though it resented being driven while so severely mauled, made for the British lines. Presently the Germans came within range of the British anti-aircraft guns, whereupon they promptly turned tail, leaving Filley to go on his way unmolested to a graceful landing which he soon was able to make.

For his courageous part in this brilliant combat Lieutenant Filley was awarded the Military Cross.

The same coveted decoration was awarded to Lieutenant W. R. Freeman (Manchester Regiment and R.F.C.) for his "gallantry, ability, and very valuable work," about the same time and in somewhat similar circumstances. Hidden German batteries had been making things decidedly uncomfortable in a certain part of the British line, and the lieutenant was detailed to reconnoitre their position. Despite continual attempts to bring him down, the lieutenant held on his way over the German lines until he succeeded in 'spotting' the guns. His machine was fitted with wireless transmitting apparatus, and he proceeded to send back the results of his observations, until at last the British artillery got the range to a nicety.

Hovering over the German lines Lieutenant Freeman had some exciting moments. All about him shells were bursting and rifle bullets came thick and fast. German aeroplanes were not absent either, but for five solid hours the aviator stuck to the task allotted to him, and, although his propeller and his planes were damaged by bullets, he refused to be driven off until he considered that his work was done. Only then did he make for his base, no doubt highly pleased with what he had achieved.

Another 'spotter,' Second-Lieutenant A. A. Benjamin Thomson (Royal Warwicks and R.F.C.), earned the Military Cross at Neuve-Chapelle in 1915. He was working in conjunction with a heavy gun which, well behind the front line, was bombarding the German trenches. On August 29th the rain was coming down in torrents and the clouds were at 500 feet only, which naturally involved flying, for observation work, at a height which was distinctly uncomfortable from several points of view. In some way, perhaps, the clouds may have proved friendly, for, when the German fire became too hot for safety, the lieutenant could dart above a cloud-bank and remain sheltered—to come through at a different spot and so compel the enemy to readjust sights and go to the trouble of getting the new range; all of which meant that the observer was given time to make his notes and send messages to the big gun, which, owing to his excellent work, was registering direct hits in quick succession.

Once, however, the clouds nearly brought disaster. Even we who grovel on *terra firma* will understand that it can be no easy matter to keep one's bearings in mid-air when, owing to a driving rain, one can scarcely see the ground below, and when one gets tucked away among thick clouds it is easy to overshoot the mark. This is what Lieutenant Thomson did. He had got in among clouds which hid everything from his sight, and when he finally came down out of them, he found himself well over the German trenches. He was quickly espied by the enemy, and a very tornado of fire instantly enveloped him. Lieutenant Thomson, however, favoured by the gods who guard the brave, lived through the storm and succeeded in driving his machine back toward our lines, over which he calmly hovered, continuing his observations, with the result that, in the course of a couple of hours, the British heavy gun tossed no fewer than ten big shells plump on to the required target, to say nothing of others which fell uncomfortably near. The discomfited Germans shook angry fists at the airman who seemed, as he hovered lightly in the grey dome of heaven, to be mocking them. It was only when it became too dark to see anything that Lieutenant Thomson volplaned to earth, after a most satisfactory piece of work.

Another aviator who, by all the rules, ought to have given up, but who succeeded by a tremendous effort in keeping his machine in action, was Second-Lieutenant Malcolm Henderson (4th Ross Highland Seaforth Highlanders, R.F.C.). This officer was accompanied by an observer who was to take photographs of enemy positions. This work naturally involved flying at a low altitude at certain places, in order to avoid clouds and the 'Archibalds,' which latter saw to it that the British aeroplane did not have an unmolested trip.

Whenever Henderson dived or spiralled into view, German anti-aircraft guns banged away at him, woolly puffs of smoke burst all round, and high explosive shells crashed thunderously above the roar of the engine.

Coolly Henderson controlled his machine, and just as calmly the observer took his photographs, and it seemed that, despite the terrific bombardment to which they were subjected, the two aviators would succeed in their mission.

Then came catastrophe.

At one place the Germans below had the range almost to an inch, and explosions of the shells made the aeroplane plunge madly. The pilot kept his head, but expected that a missile would strike home at any moment. He did not have long to wait. Suddenly the machine staggered, and seemed as though it would turn over; there was a deafening roar, a tearing, ripping sound, followed by another, a hoarse cry from the pilot, a startled exclamation from the observer. For an instant the machine hung, as it were, out of control, then gave a downward lurch. The slip might have ended in a nosedive but for the pilot's tremendous reassertion of self-control. After recovering from the first shock of the appalling thing that had happened, Henderson set himself a task which was sufficient to daunt, so one would think, the bravest of men.

What had happened in that dramatic moment was this: a gun had found the exact range and a shell, hitting the nacelle of the aeroplane, had crashed its way through the floor, cut off one of Henderson's legs just below the knee, and then continued on its way into space.

Losing blood as he was at a fearful rate, with his head dizzy, his eyes bleared, every nerve affected by the shock, who could have blamed Lieutenant Henderson if he had given up? How could any man be expected to withstand so awful a disaster? In all too many cases, such a tragedy must have resulted in a still greater one, the culmination being a wrecked and burning machine, the funeral pyre of its occupants.

But incredible as it may seem, the dramatic truth is that the heroic Henderson on regaining consciousness immediately got his machine under control again while at that dizzy height of 7000 feet, and with the one determination to save his aeroplane, his observer, and the precious photographs, set his course toward the British lines.

Meantime, the German gunners, whose observers had marked the effect of the shell, had fully expected to see the machine fall crashing to the ground, but when, to their amazement, it recovered equilibrium and then turned round and made off, they feverishly got to work again. But ere they had made up their minds to act, Henderson had driven his 'plane so far that it was necessary for the artillery to get a new range, and by the time that was done he was still farther off. With a deafening roar the engine drove the 'plane along at its giddy height, and with physical strength fast waning, and the strain sapping his nervous energy, the pilot manipulated his machine, dodging the Teuton's 'woolly bears' when the range was too accurate to be pleasant. Already in the distance he could see the British lines, and if only consciousness would last, safety was assured. Bracing himself for a last effort, Henderson set his teeth, and, holding gamely on through the pursuing shells, he presently volplaned to earth well within our own lines. Only then did his grip relax and his senses leave him.

Chapter 2

Some Stories of 'Rupert'

Although we hear more about the aeroplane than we do about the kite balloon, it must not be forgotten that the former has by no means ousted the latter from its place as a valuable arm in an army's equipment. The aeroplane goes out over the enemy's lines, seeking hidden batteries, photographing positions, locating reserves, and hovering over bombarded sectors and signalling to the far-off gunners the effect of their firing. The balloon—that is, the kite balloon, the queer-looking, unwieldy gas-bag with its observation car dangling below—is used behind the lines continuously to observe the effect of gunfire; but, although it is behind the lines, it is by no means safe. Why, by the way, the kite balloon should have been christened 'Rupert' no one knows, any more than it is possible to find out why the anti-aircraft gun should be called 'Archibald,' but there it is. Wherever the flying men go they carry their 'lingo' with them, and, no doubt, these Uttle things give a touch of humour to what is, after all, a most serious business.

Naturally, the artillery objects to enemy kite balloons, and attempts are made to bring them down—both by gunfire and aeroplane attacks. As a result, many have gone to earth in flames, and lucky is the observation officer in such circumstances who escapes with his life. Very often, when a strong wind is blowing, the cables cannot stand the strain put upon them, the balloon tugs like a dog on the leash, shakes itself, and goes on a wild, free voyage at the bidding of the wind—sometimes toward the enemy's lines.

An incident of this latter kind befell Second-Lieutenant A. C. D. Gavin (Royal Highlanders and R.F.C.) and a passenger who was in the swaying car with him. A bombardment was about to take place at a certain point of the line, and Lieutenant Gavin had been deputed to go aloft. The great gas-bag, unwieldy, hideous-looking thing that it was, had been inflated, and the lieutenant and his passenger took their places in the basket. The word was given to be off; strong-armed men on a motor lorry nearby began to unwind a steel cable from a big winch, and the 'Rupert' started to mount, swaying in the wind, but always being brought back to position by the queer-looking 'rudder.' Up and up, until, at 4000 feet, the balloon came to rest—if continually straining at a leash which will not allow the balloon to go higher can be called rest.

Far below, and well away from the motor lorry, the guns were firing. Lieutenant Gavin through his binoculars marked where the shells burst in the distant German lines. Presently there was a great spout of earth and debris of all kinds. The lieutenant spoke a few words into the telephone with which his balloon was provided, and the man in the shelter below received a message which told of the result of that trial round; he in turn telephoned it to the far-off battery, the receiver there rushed off to the officer in charge, the range was altered, and once again the heavies opened fire.

Meanwhile, up in the basket, Lieutenant Gavin was having no pleasant time. The Germans had quickly realized that the good marksmanship being made by the battery they could not see and could not hit was the result of the keen watching of the man in the swaying basket, and they were doing their utmost to bring his observation work to a close. They opened fire with their heavies, aided by their own balloonists, who knew that beneath the British balloon there was the attendant lorry, and this being a better target than the gas-bag itself, they directed their gunners' fire toward it. Lieutenant Gavin, looking down, saw a 'crump' arrive, saw the earth flung up in a shower, and knew that he was likely to be cut adrift. While yet his cables held, however, he was going to carry out the work assigned to him, and, all unconcerned, as became a Briton, he went calmly on with the task of correcting the range of our own firing and noting the effect of the shells.

Observation work is not all plain sailing. The Germans have a little dodge which they play, and that is to fire off flashes at various points, hoping to mislead the observer into believing that they are the flashes of guns. A man needs to be well trained and well experienced to avoid being fooled in this way, because to be deceived means that the battery will waste hundreds of shells, perhaps, on trying to smash guns which do not exist!

Lieutenant Gavin was not to be deceived, and he did such good work that the Germans realized that unless they made better practice with their firing their guns would be out-matched. So they concentrated upon the lorry; there was a terrific roar below, the balloon gave a sudden leap upward; and, looking down, the lieutenant saw a great hole in the ground where the lorry had once stood.

He knew what had happened, and he knew that his work for that day, at any rate, if not for the duration of the war, was over. The balloon, as though happy to be released, bounded still higher, and, caught in a wind current, began to drift toward the enemy's lines!

Such a moment calls for prompt action, and Lieutenant Gavin was not found wanting. Dropping many hundreds of feet in a parachute does not appeal to everybody, and many can remember the feeling of dread at exhibitions when the parachutist dropped out of the basket of his balloon and a violent death seemed to be assured.

Perhaps parachuting is a fine sport, if you know how to use the apparatus; but if you have not. been initiated, there is little sport about it, especially if shrapnel is screaming around. However, Lieutenant Gavin coolly set to work to instruct his passenger in the use of the parachute, made sure that he understood, then, with a cheery *au revoir*, helped him up on to the edge of the basket, which was swaying perilously all the time, and told him to "Go!" The passenger obeyed the injunction and dropped like a plummet for innumerable feet. His heart must have been in his mouth no doubt, and he must have wondered whether the wretched envelope would ever open.

Gavin now had no time to waste. Before he could follow his passenger on the exciting trip, there was much to be done. Supposing the balloon came down in the enemy's territory the Germans must not get hold of the valuable papers in the basket. These papers contained confidential instructions, and his own elaborate observations for the eyes of the staff only. There were also instruments the secrets of which were not to be surrendered to the enemy.

Gavin hastily gathered his papers, and deliberately destroyed them what time the current of wind was carrying the balloon swiftly toward the German lines. At last the final piece of paper was torn to shreds, the instruments were smashed beyond recognition; and then, and then only, did Gavin think about himself. He looked down out of the basket, and saw that he was still over the British lines, but rapidly approaching their limits. He seized his parachute, saw that it was in working order, put himself into the ring, gripped the handholds provided, climbed upon the edge of the basket, noted the white covering of his comrade's parachute still dropping toward earth—and fell, like Lucifer, into the emptiness below.

Would the envelope never open? Was that terrific rush to keep on until he smashed into the ground? And, if the parachute did open, where would he land?

Gavin could not answer all of those questions at once. The answer to the first came suddenly: there was a jerk at his arms, as though they were being pulled out of their sockets, then the downward mad rush ceased, and in its place there was a gentle floating motion. He would not crash into the ground! From below, as he drew nearer, came the louder boom of guns; presently came the rattle of machine-gun fire, and he realized that he was just over the front lines. But in which front lines would he land?

Down and down he continued to drop, his field of vision becoming narrower as he neared the earth; the white lines of chalk which he knew to be trenches grew clearer and more distinct, and at last he knew that he would land where he wanted to land—within the British lines.

However, when he touched earth German machine-guns were rattling perilously, and he had good reason to thank his lucky stars when at last he crawled unharmed into a British trench.

On a day toward the end of 1916, during a tremendous bombardment by both sides, Second-Lieutenant Norman Brearley (Liverpool Regiment and R.F.C.) decided that a certain 'Rupert' well behind the German lines was proving far too useful, and he resolved to bring its career to an end. As he winged his way over the front lines toward his objective the Lieutenant chuckled at the thought of the surprise he was going to give the Huns—always supposing that a certain little ruse he had in mind proved workable.

Long before he arrived anywhere near the 'Rupert,' he was spotted, and the 'Archies' did their best to drive him back or bring him down. But Lieutenant Brearley was a 'sticker,' and held on his way until, with 'woolly bears' woofing all about him, he was immediately above the kite balloon. The anti-aircraft guns, of course, redoubled their efforts, while the observers in the basket of the balloon fired madly from their rifles.

Suddenly the Germans on *terra firma* shouted excitedly; the tiny speck in the sky was seen to be in trouble, apparently having been winged.

What had happened?

A high explosive shell had burst near the aeroplane, the machine had suddenly tilted, and with its planes almost at right angles to the ground had begun to side-slip at an amazing speed. Not one of the Germans below thought that anything could save the airman. Great was the rejoicing among the gunners, while the occupants of the 'Rupert' felt that they had been saved from a fate they scarcely dared think about.

The 'Archies' stopped firing, for it was only throwing away good ammunition to pursue a stricken foe whose life was all but spent.

Lieutenant Brearley sat tight, but there was no fear in his face, nothing about him that would have suggested that he knew he was hurtling to his death: instead a grim smile lurked about his mouth and a determined look was in his eyes as his hand gripped the trigger of his Lewis gun.

For this side-slip down through space was not the result of the machine being hit at all; it was a deliberate manoeuvre! The ruse was not one to be lightly attempted, for in order to deceive the spectators below, the machine must drop sheer with wings vertical and at a terrific speed to give the appearance that it was out of control. The trick called for grit—called for a man who was willing to take his life in his hands, because it might easily be that the machine could not be righted in time and then

But Lieutenant Brearley was willing to risk all in order to bring 'Rupert' down, and the machine slipped speedily through the air, dropping thousands of feet in an incredibly short time to 1500 feet from the ground, when it was almost level with the balloon, which was now being hauled down.

Then the amazing thing happened.

The enemy below saw the apparently doomed machine suddenly right itself and, in a flash, dive straight for the unwieldy envelope. Too late it was realized that things were not what they seemed and that the Briton had been playing a trick. The guns opened out immediately, but 'Rupert' was now acting as a shield to the intrepid airman, whose machine-gun was firing rapidly upon it.

Meanwhile the Germans were striving to haul down their balloon before the aviator could inflict deadly injury upon it, but as he was provided with an efficient weapon for such an attack and was no prentice hand at the work, it was not long before Lieutenant Brearley had the satisfaction of seeing the ugly mass go blazing to earth, utterly destroyed.

Then, as the official account notifying an award of the Military Cross for the brilliant deed says, "he returned."

CHAPTER 3

Some Fine British Raids

It is an undisputed fact that the British Flying Services have carried out some of the largest raids in the course of the war, and there have been so many of them that it is impossible to describe everyone here. It is worth remembering that these raids differed from those undertaken by the Germans when their airships visited Britain: our raids are always against places of military importance, whereas the world knows the object of German frightfulness.

Quite early in the conflict our airmen, in twos and threes—and sometimes more—went on long-distance flights, to attack some important point behind the German lines, as, for instance, when Squadron-Commander Spenser Grey, and Lieutenants S.V. Sippe and Marix, of the R.N.A.S., on October 8th, 1914, sailed over the airship shed at Düsseldorf, dropped bombs which hit their mark and set fire to the shed and the Zeppelin inside, as they plainly saw by the tall pillar of smoke and flame which arose immediately after the bombs struck.

Then, on November 21st of the same year, there was a daring aerial attack on the Zeppelin works at Friedrichshafen, on the shores of Lake Constance, where Count Zeppelin built the giant gasbags which were to be used on murder raids. The flying men who took part in the attack on the works were Squadron-Commander E. F. Briggs, Flight-Commander J. E. Babbington, and Flight-Lieutenant S.V. Sippe, who set out from an aerodrome in the neighbourhood of Belfort, their Avro machines, driven by 80-horse-power Gnomes, humming their way up until they were but mere specks in the sky. The course taken lay to the north of the frontier of Switzerland, and Friedrichshafen was sighted about midday.

The success with which the airmen steered toward their objective made the Germans realize that British aviators were not to be despised as the "contemptible little army" had been; and yet, rather than admit this, the enemy avowed that the raid had only been possible by reason of the fact that our diplomats in Switzerland had improperly given information which had assisted the aviators; which was another German lie that needed no refutation. What had happened was that the Britons had studied the problem and had made themselves masters of the route they were going to take, with the result that they surprised the Germans at Friedrichshafen, who had never expected such an attack from the air.

One of the airmen got lost temporarily in a bank of cloud, but Commander Briggs and his other companion dropped to the attack in a giddy volplane. Coming directly over the works they loosed their bombs, and the crash of the explosions mingled with the roar of firing guns, the sharp bark of rifles and the *tat-tat-tat* of machine-guns—all of which the Germans turned upon the daring aviators, who swept round in wide circles, their planes riddled by the bullets. When the third airman emerged from the cloud-bank he saw that his commander was in trouble: his machine was dropping. An unlucky bullet had pierced the petrol tank, the engine petered out, and the gallant pilot knew that he would have to descend. He kept his head, however, and maintained control over his mount until he had brought it to a graceful landing near the devastated works. A crowd of Germans immediately surrounded him, and their appearance was so threatening that the commander drew his revolver, thus keeping at bay the angry foe, who did not know that the revolver was empty! In due course a German officer came up and Commander Briggs surrendered, not a little mortified that his successful attack should have come to such an inglorious end.

Meanwhile, his two comrades were hurrying home, for the necessities of war decreed that they must leave the commander to the mercy of the enemy. One who described this affair at the time wrote:

> If they had come unperceived they were not to leave the country without risk. The news of their presence was telegraphed from town to town; motorcars mounting machine-guns and anti-aircraft cannon were dispatched at full speed to the most likely points; observers were specially detailed to watch the Swiss border and to note whether these adventurers crossed the frontier. But such was the extraordinary speed with which the airmen returned, that scarcely had the news of their arrival

been received than the airmen themselves were over the place to which communication had been made and were out of sight before any effective step could be taken to intercept them.

When the airmen reached the flying ground near Belfort they received a hearty and enthusiastic welcome, and later they were decorated with the Legion of Honour.

Cuxhaven, the German war port situate at the mouth of the river Elbe and protected to seaward by the great fortress of Heligoland, had its first experience of modern war on the morning of Christmas Day 1914, when a number of British seaplanes appeared out of the mist and dropped bombs upon its ship-building yards and fortifications.

This raid, the first that the Royal Naval Air Service had undertaken from the sea, was extremely well planned. There were seven seaplanes, which were borne out to sea by two new seaplane carriers, one an erstwhile cross-Channel steamer which had been converted into an auxiliary war-vessel. These two ships were escorted by several submarines, two destroyer flotillas, and the new light cruiser *Arethusa*, which, before she met with her untimely end in 1916, was to add to the many laurels gained by the long list of 'saucy *Arethusas*' in the annals of the British Navy.

While on their mother-ships the seaplanes, which were Short tractors, had their wings folded up; when the appointed rendezvous was reached, the machines were lowered over the side into the water, their planes were opened, their engines began to roar, and having driven through the water the distance required to get up sufficient speed to allow of rising, up through the mist they soared, droning on their way to their objective. The seven pilots engaged in the dashing adventure were Flight-Commanders Oliver, Hewlett, Kilner and Ross, Flight-Lieutenants Miley and Edmonds, and Flight-Sub-Lieutenant Gaskell Blackburn, each of whom was an experienced airman.

Day was just breaking when the seaplanes whirred upward, leaving their escorts to move seaward to await their return from what was to prove a hazardous adventure. If the British anticipated that they would be unmolested they were quickly disillusioned, for not long after the seaplanes had left their mother-ships a squadron of enemy 'planes, accompanied by a Zeppelin, appeared and bore down toward the British machines, which, however, held on their way, knowing that the destroyers and the *Arethusa* would deal with the coming foes. The *Arethusa*, provided as she was with special anti-aircraft artillery, was a formidable adversary, as the Zeppelin soon discovered, for, directly the airship was sighted, the gunners on the cruiser opened fire with such accuracy and at such a rate that the aerial monster was compelled to swing round and beat a hasty retreat.

Meanwhile, the German seaplanes, which naturally did not present such good targets to anti-aircraft guns, kept on their course toward the ships, arrived over them, and began dropping bombs, which fell so close to the vessels that on many occasions the water-spouts which were flung up as the result of the explosions broke and tumbled in cascades upon the decks. Fortunately, however, not a single bomb struck a ship, and the rapid gunfire that was maintained rendered the situation so uncomfortable for the seaplanes that they turned tail and made for their base.

While this strange battle between aircraft and seacraft was in progress, the British seaplanes were winging their way through the fog to Cuxhaven. Arrived there, they dropped their bombs and did a certain amount of damage, made their observations—which were the chief motive for the raid—and then swept round and flew seaward. Everything had been put upon a time schedule, which was so accurately adhered to that even while the enemy 'planes were still hovering over the British destroyers the raiders reappeared. Some of them swooped down to the sea, and taxied along the surface to where they knew that submarines were awaiting them. Immediately the conning-tower of the underwater craft appeared the nearest seaplane came to a standstill, the pilot unstrapped himself, and stood ready with knife in hand to rip up the great floats of his machine.

When the conning-tower opened, and a naval officer appeared, the destructive work was carried out and the seaplane, costing over £1000, began to sink rapidly and was almost submerged by the time that the pilot had been taken into the submarine, which immediately dived beneath the surface. It may seem a wasteful method, but in war money must be sacrificed for the sake of that which is more precious; in this case the information which the pilots had gleaned far outweighed in value the cost of the machines which it had been necessary to destroy.

Four of the pilots were rescued by submarines in the manner described, but two who returned in the van of their comrades alighted on the surface near the seaplane carriers, to whose sides they taxied even while the enemy aircraft were still dropping their bombs. It was an occasion for some prompt work on the part of the men aboard. To

The British Air Raid on Cuxhaven, Christmas Day 1914

enable them to pick up the seaplanes it was necessary for the two ships to come to a standstill and so render themselves much better marks for the enemy bombs; they stopped, nevertheless, hoists were swung out, and the machines were picked up as they taxied alongside. A moment later the keen-eyed commanders, who were in constant communication with their engine rooms, rang down for "Full steam ahead!" the ships trembled to the thrust of their engines, then leapt through the water, making for home.

There was one thing that marred the success of the enterprise, and that was that only six out of the seven intrepid pilots had been picked up, and the escorting vessels, knowing how risky it was to linger, had to steam away without the missing aviator. This was Flight-Commander Hewlett, who, as it afterward transpired, had an exceedingly adventurous time. The thick fog which enveloped the seaplanes greatly bothered Hewlett, and he lost his way, although after a long time he succeeded in reaching Cuxhaven. Arriving as he did after his comrades had left, he naturally received a very warm welcome from the Germans, who were now on the *qui vive*, not knowing whether more of the daring airmen would appear. To make matters worse, the flight-commander, owing to the fog, had to fly low, so low, in fact, that as he swept over the war port he almost touched the tall masts of the ships lying at anchor in the harbour.

As soon as he had located his position, Hewlett set his machine to climb out of danger, dropping bombs as he went, and followed by a perfect hail of shells from every anti-aircraft gun within range. He knew that at any moment his upward sweep might be changed into a plunge to death, and the firing was so vigorous that he quite expected this to happen. Fortunately, however, either the German gunners were bad marksmen or else the fog which had baffled the airman was now interfering with the aim of the artillerymen; whatever the reason, no shell touched Hewlett's machine and no bullet found a resting-place in his body. Up and still up, and headed seaward, the seaplane flew, and the commander was beginning to think that the Fates were not altogether unkind when something went wrong with his engine, which began to backfire and ultimately stopped.

This was indeed a tragedy. Commander Hewlett's one hope was that he might not have missed the escort. As he planed down to the grey, tossing sea, he scanned the horizon in search of a friendly ship, but none appeared, and he realized that, not having kept to the scheduled time, he had had to be left by the destroyers.

When his floats touched water the airman was in anything but a comfortable frame of mind. Neither of the possible alternatives—one of which was that he might stay there until the floats became so water-logged that they would not support the machine, in which case he would be drowned, and the other that an enemy ship might appear and take him prisoner—was at all cheering. It was all very disappointing, after having escaped from the inferno of Cuxhaven!

The airman, sitting in his machine and rocked to and fro at the bidding of the wind and waves, peered for a long and weary time through the mist, hoping against hope that he might be rescued. When he had almost ceased to expect succour, the dark bows of a trawler appeared out of the mist, scattering the spray as she came. The stranded airman on the derelict seaplane—for by this time the machine was in a sorry plight—signalled for help; happily the lookout on the trawler saw him, and the vessel bore down upon the spot. The trawler proved to be Dutch, which from Hewlett's point of view was not so good as if it had been British, but by no means so bad as if it had been German.

It did not take long to make the trawler's captain understand what had happened, and, having scuttled his machine, Hewlett was taken on board the fishing vessel and carried to Holland.

The fact of his being taken into Holland raised a question of international law, which has laid it down that any member of the fighting services of a belligerent nation taking refuge in a neutral country shall be interned during the progress of the war. Commander Hewlett, however, set up the plea that this law did not apply to him, because he was a shipwrecked mariner who had been rescued out at sea. There was, of course, much argument, but in the end the airman's plea was accepted, he was released, and in due course returned to England.

Thus every one of the daring raiders returned safely, and, considering how successful they had been both in bombing and in gathering information, the raid on Cuxhaven may be said to have been a complete triumph.

What was at that date probably the longest official report of one exploit in the air was that which was issued by the Admiralty dealing with a very satisfactory raid on February 11th, 1915. The report ran:

> During the last twenty-four hours combined aeroplane and seaplane operations have been carried out by the Naval Wing in the Bruges, Zeebrugge, Blankenberghe and Ostend districts, with a view to preventing the development of submarine bases

and establishments.

Thirty-four naval aeroplanes and seaplanes took part.

Great damage is reported to have been done to Ostend Railway Station, which, according to present information, has probably been burnt to the ground. The railway station at Blankenberghe was damaged and railway lines were torn up in many places.

Bombs were dropped on gun positions at Middelkerke, also on the power-station and German mine-sweeping vessels at Zeebrugge, but the damage is unknown.

During the attack the machines encountered heavy banks of snow.

No submarines were seen.

Flight-Commander Grahame-White fell into the sea off Nieuport and was rescued by a French vessel.

Although exposed to heavy gunfire from rifles, anti-aircraft guns, *mitrailleuses*, etc., all pilots are safe. Two machines were damaged.

The seaplanes and aeroplanes were under the command of Wing-Commander Samson, assisted by Wing-Commander Longmore and Squadron-Commanders Porte, Courtney, and Rathbone.

The very length of that *communiqué* suggests that the operations were on a large scale and regarded as important, while behind the official language there is hidden a thrilling story, which will someday be told in full. Meanwhile, we have only glimpses, the best of which is that given in a letter from Flight-Lieutenant Harold Rosher, R.N.A.S., who took part in the raid.

The machines left their base on Wednesday morning, the 10th of February, at intervals of two minutes, the slowest machines going first. Driving into the mist they hummed across the Channel, with an escort of destroyers below. The farther they went the denser the mist became, the clouds were very heavy, and they ran into a driving snowstorm which utterly baffled them. The aviators had instructions to land at Dunkirk if the weather conditions were such that they could not reach their objectives, and when they arrived off the French coast it was evident to all of them that it would be Dunkirk for that day, whatever the morrow might bring forth. They did not give in without a struggle, however, and pushed along the coast until it was impossible and imprudent to proceed any farther. Grahame-White, as we have seen, had to come down in the sea, where he waited in his machine until he was picked up. It had been a most exciting trip across Channel, even although a disheartening one. Flight-Lieutenant Rosher's experience was probably typical of many others. He wrote:[1]

> The clouds got thicker and my compass became useless, swinging round and round, I was about 7000 feet up and absolutely lost. The next thing I realized was that my speed-indicator had rushed up to *ninety miles* an hour and the wind was fairly whistling through the wires. I pulled her up, but had quite lost control.
>
> A hair-raising experience followed. I nosedived, side-slipped, stalled [lost speed], etc. etc., time after time, my speed varying from practically nothing up to over 100 miles an hour. I kept my head, but was absolutely scared stiff. I didn't get out of the clouds, which lower down turned into a snow-storm and hail, until I was only 1500 feet up. I came out diving headlong for the earth.

By brilliant skill the aviator righted his machine, and he tried his utmost to get out of the snowstorm, skirt it and drive inland. Failing in this he then endeavoured to get beneath the storm, but was again unsuccessful. Realizing at last that he could not hope to accomplish his purpose he turned back for Dunkirk, where he found the rest of the party except one, presumably Grahame-White.

It was a crowd of pretty 'sick' aviators which assembled at Dunkirk that day, but all were determined that the Germans should feel the weight of the bombs which had been brought over for their especial benefit, and early the following morning the airmen were ready to take up the interrupted task. It was dark and misty and cloudy when the machines ascended and set out seaward to get as far off the shore as possible and thus be out of range of the anti-aircraft batteries, which began a wild song of hate as soon as the droning of the engines was heard below.

At Ostend the raiders were bombarded from scores of guns, but this did not prevent them loosing their destructive missiles, and they sailed on, leaving a trail of disaster behind. Flight-Lieutenant Rosher was among the party bound for Zeebrugge, and when they arrived there, the cloud-banks were so low that they had to let go their bombs when at a height of only 5500 feet. This, of course, gave the Germans

---
1. *With the Flying Squadron* by Harold Rosher also published by Leonaur.

a great opportunity, and their shrapnel burst all around, fortunately, however, without result. The shipping in the docks was struck by the British bombs, and the power-station burst into flame as the aviators winged their way across, and so out to sea.

Considering that the German gunners, who had had a good deal of experience against our raiding machines, were, as Lieutenant Rosher said, hitting at 8000 feet and reckoned on getting every third shot home, it says much for the skill of the British pilots that they all returned safely, well pleased with themselves at having given the enemy something to remember. But in case they might forget, on February 16th, the Naval Wing returned and distributed a plentiful supply of bombs over very much the same area as before. In this great raid there were forty machines engaged, the Ostend and Middelkerke batteries were bombed, transport wagons on the Ostend-Ghistelles road were shattered, the mole and locks of Zeebrugge were further damaged, and the shipping off Blankenberghe and Zeebrugge suffered heavily.

While the British aviators were thus engaged on these points of importance, eight French machines, together with some British naval 'planes, swooped over to the Ghistelles aerodrome, on which they made a vigorous attack, so keeping the German airmen too busily employed to allow them to wing their way coastward to cut off the raiders, some of whom, nevertheless, fell victims to the enemy.

One of the largest raids undertaken by British machines was that on March 18th, 1916, when fifty British machines attacked the German aerodrome near Ostend and the submarine base at Zeebrugge. Had it been daylight when the raiders started there would have been a rare sight for spectators as the fifty machines spluttered their way over the flying ground and bounded up into the air one after the other. It was night, however and nothing was to be seen except the occasional flash as pilots switched on their torches to indicate to comrades the direction being taken. With these intermittent lights to guide them the squadron formed into a V-shaped flight, with the bombing machines tucked in the centre and the fighting Moranes on the flanks, ready to tackle any enemy 'planes which might endeavour to head off the raiders.

The airmen sped over the dunes, with the sea gleaming below them and the subdued lights of Ostend in the distance ahead, and in due course divided into two parties, one making for Ostend, the other stealing through the night toward Zeebrugge. The attack on Ostend came as a complete surprise to the Germans there, and the aeroplane hangar felt the force of British explosives: resounding roars came to the airmen, who saw the flames belching from hangar and storehouses. The German flying men, taken by surprise, dashed for cover, leaving their aeroplanes burning merrily.

Meanwhile, the Zeebrugge party had also reached their objective, having safely passed the anti-aircraft batteries, with whose positions they were conversant, seeing that all the pilots had made a careful study of the stretch of coast over which they had flown, and knew just where the batteries were placed. In the docks at Zeebrugge were many German destroyers and submarines, and at the first crash of exploding bombs something in the nature of a panic ensued. Destroyers hurried out to sea, where monitors awaited them; submarines dived quickly to escape the falling bombs; soldiers and marines on shore darted for cover, although many of them—two hundred, it was reckoned at the time—were killed.

It was a scene of terror for the Germans; the bombs fell in quick succession as the aeroplanes followed one another over the docks, and so far as could be gathered afterward a tremendous amount of damage was done, which is not surprising, considering that during the raid on the naval base and aerodrome some ten thousand pounds of high explosives were distributed! The men who took part were to be congratulated upon the effectiveness of their work, and it was probably due to the important results achieved that a week later the attempt was made upon the Zeppelin bases on the Sylt island, off Schleswig-Holstein, of which we have to tell in Chapter 6.

We have by no means exhausted the list of important raids, but the instances given are more or less typical of most of the others. Sometimes all the aviators returned, at others some were brought down or had to descend through engine trouble; in nearly every case, however, the raiders succeeded in their purpose, while the constant harassing of the enemy at strategic and important points served to keep him in mind of the efficiency of the British Flying Services.

CHAPTER 4

The Pluck of Major Brabazon Rees

The 'wasp' hummed through the air, and the goggled pilot, engaged on work which ought to go through without interruption, scanned the surrounding space for signs of possible foes. Finding none, he took in all details that he could of what was going on below. It seemed that the trip was going to be a fairly comfortable one, a 'joy-ride' almost, and Major Lionel Wilmot Brabazon Rees, R.A., R.F.C., was not at all worried. The calmness, however, was destined to be disturbed suddenly by one of those terrific events which take place so unexpectedly in the air.

Far off, in the misty distance, driving toward the British lines, there presently appeared a little bunch of black spots which, to any but a man whose eyes had been trained to see, might have been taken, perhaps, for the dancing, mocking dots which are to many the signs of indigestion; but Major Rees, practised aviator as he was, who had fought and won many an aerial duel, knew that those black spots were aeroplanes.

Earlier in the day, as the major knew, a party of British fliers had droned over the German lines to harass enemy communications, and, as far as he knew, had not returned.

The appearance of the darting black spots in the direction from which the raiders would come on their return caused Major Rees to believe that they were the homing birds of the Flying Corps, and as there was little else doing just then, the gallant and courteous pilot let his engine all out and went up to meet the approaching machines, intending to escort them home, and, if necessary, to fight off any Germans who ventured to try to intercept them.

Then Major Rees made a startling discovery: the gradually approaching dots resolved themselves into no fewer than ten machines driving along in good formation, and, to the surprise of the major, when they were close enough to be distinguished through his binoculars, he saw on their wings, not the tricoloured circle of the Allies, but the sinister black cross of the Hun.

And those ten machines, the pilots of which had sighted the lonely patrol, were opening out as they came in order to surround him from above and below, from front and rear, from left side and right side.

The gallant major, when he discovered his mistake, did not bank and go swinging round for home, but went boldly forward, to join issue with the foremost of the enemy. The machines met, and while the remainder of the foe were flying like carrion crows to the feast, the two fought out a light which, although short, was bitter and fierce. The vicious Lewis gun barked in anger at the Nordenfeldt, and a hail of shots spattered through the rival machines and made grim music, which each of the aviators knew might end in the crash of a *grande finale*.

With a roar. Major Rees' machine swept under the German, followed a sharp wheel, and the Britisher was mounting to the attack again, to be in turn sprayed by a stream of bullets. In this manner for a brief space of time, into which was crowded all the terror of aerial fighting, the 'scrap' went on, until Major Rees realized that his opponent's fire had slackened, whereupon, driving into him, he sent the Hun diving to the ground, not mortally wounded, but so badly mauled that it was impossible for him to continue the fight.

So rapidly had the conflict been waged and ended that it was all over and the German was slipping down the dizzy heights before his companions could get near enough to give much assistance. As it was, when they saw the plight of their comrade, five of them, while yet at a long range, opened fire with their machine-guns, and five hail-storms seemed to break upon the British pilot's machine.

Major Rees, scorning to fly from even such superior numbers, sailed into closer quarters, singled out a foe, and after another stiff, sharp fight drove him off, then turned upon another and treated him in a similar way.

Such doughty fighting, whirlwind tactics of a sort that enabled the British pilot to fight and conquer and come up again, completely demoralized the other three Germans, who, thinking discretion the better part of valour, now scattered and made off, bent upon getting out of range of the British fire-eater.

Major Rees, his machine showing many signs of the mauling it

The R.F.C. at work
Aerial action at an altitude of two and a quarter miles between four British machines and nine German

had received, breathed more freely when he saw his enemies beating their retreat. Not that he was afraid, but the respite gave him a breathing space in which to see what damage had been done to his machine. He found that it was still workable and under control, for which he was glad, because westward he could see a couple of cross-marked aeroplanes going full out, and being in fighting mood. Major Rees hurried on their trail.

The German aviators swung round the nozzles of their snappy little weapons, to point clear at the Britisher, who, with his own Lewis unshipped, was rapidly coming up. The two streams of shot whistled through the air and the Germans' bullets broke upon and through the major's nacelle and wings. One of the Germans, when the distance had lessened, succeeded in getting into an advantageous position—a momentary advantage, but yet just enough for what he had in mind: his machine-gun kept up its *staccato rat-tat*, and some of the bullets plugged their way into his adversary's thigh. Under the shock of the impact Major Rees temporarily lost control. His machine slipped in the way that aeroplanes do when the guiding brain no longer controls them, made a quick dart forward, and then fell sheer down at a terrifying speed.

It seemed that there was nothing but disaster awaiting Major Rees.

In such moments everything depends upon the man, and in this case the man was not found wanting. Faint from loss of blood, with a sharp stinging pain in his thigh, and with the knowledge that unless he acted promptly and coolly he would be dashed to death below, Major Rees, while the machine spun, succeeded by a miraculous effort in getting the 'plane in hand once more. There was quick work with the 'joy-stick' and rudder-bar, and suddenly the machine, which a second before seemed doomed, had righted itself and was going on, and, wonder of wonders—its pilot was driving for his foes!

Close in he drove his 'plane, so close that only a few yards separated the combatants, and the major could see the begoggled faces of the Germans. At this close range Major Rees expended his ammunition, drum after drum, until at last not a bullet remained. The report which notified the award of the Victoria Cross to him says:

> Then he returned home, landing his machine safely in our lines.

Already, before this, Major Rees had made for himself a reputation in the service. As early as September 21st, 1915, he had performed a deed which, among others, won for him the M.C. He was flying a one-gunned aeroplane, with Flight-Sergeant Hargreaves as companion, when he saw 2000 feet beneath him a very large German machine, mounting two machine-guns. The Hun 'plane was sweeping along at a terrific rate, and Major Rees—or as he was then. Captain Rees—knew that so far as speed was concerned, the enemy had the advantage of him. Such trifles, however, do not worry the men who gained from Sir John French the eulogy that they had won the supremacy of the air.

The major went down in a fine spiral and then dived at the foe—firing his gun as he did so and rattling bullets upon the German aeroplane, which, however, being so much faster was able to evade the down-rushing Britisher. Before the pilot could right his machine, the German had banked, turned and come up so sharply that he could get his antagonist broadside on. Instantly the machine-guns opened fire and a hurricane of bullets swept Major Rees' machine. The British gun was not idle, however, and it answered the enemy in its own way, answered so effectively that Major Rees, handling his machine with remarkable skill and cool-headedness, suddenly saw the German make a sharp turn and glide away.

One of the nickel pellets had delivered its message somewhere in the enemy's engine, and the great 'plane, apparently uncontrollable for fighting purposes, went gliding down, to land eventually just behind the German lines near Herbecourt. On another occasion the gallant major attacked a hostile aeroplane and a dramatic, hard-hitting fight took place. The foes were well matched in courage, and neither would admit defeat for some time. Major Rees, with one main spar of his machine shot through, fought on with the proverbial courage of the Briton and battered his enemy unmercifully. Not even when the stream of bullets from the German partly shattered a rear spar did the major give up, but, persisting in his attack and drawing in closer than ever, to make sure of effective firing, he succeeded in driving the enemy down.

A third enemy machine suffered as sadly at the hands of Major Rees and his companion, Flight-Sergeant Hargreaves. The Hun was no mean antagonist, but a large, speedy fighting machine, far more powerful than that piloted by the Briton, who, however, sailed into the 'scrap,' driving up, diving, banking, turning, and so on, all the time letting the German have full benefit of the Lewis gun. For three-quarters of an hour the fight went on, until, the last drum having been expended. Major Rees flew away.

The Germans must have felt very pleased that they had succeeded in driving off so stubborn an adversary, and never doubting but that they had seen the last of him, they climbed aloft, looking for more victories.

They did not know that Major Rees had gone to his aerodrome, not to take his ease after a brilliant fight, but to replenish his stock of ammunition. They were soon to learn, however, for back he now came with all the speed he could get out of his engine. A strenuous encounter followed, and this time the major was one too many for his antagonist, for soon the German machine went sliding down the unseen precipices, to crash into the unyielding ground below.

CHAPTER 5

The End of the "Königsberg"

The credit for making possible the destruction of the German raiding light cruiser *Königsberg*, without undue loss to ourselves, belongs to the men of the Royal Naval Air Service. When the war began the *Königsberg* was at Dar-es-Salaam, and, acting upon orders given long before, no doubt, she at once commenced operations against British shipping on the east coast of Africa. Among her exploits was a sudden attack on the obsolete British cruiser *Pegasus*, which, some time previously, had bombarded Dar-es-Salaam and then put in at Zanzibar to see to her rusty old boilers and generally tinker up before undertaking further work. The *Pegasus* never made another voyage, however, for on September 19th, 1914, while she was still under repair, a scathing bombardment was opened upon her, and her commander, looking seaward, saw what he recognized to be the *Königsberg*, belching flame from every gun she could bring to bear. T
he poor old *Pegasus* could not reply to any effect because her assailant was well out of range of her guns. The conclusion was foregone and the *Königsberg*, having wreaked her evil will upon the old cruiser, steamed away. But there had been some fine heroism on board the *Pegasus*, only one example of which we have space to mention here. This was the conduct of certain of the crew who, seeing their ensign shot away from the halyards, promptly made a rush for it, and, there being no other available means of restoring it, held it aloft in their hands, waving it jauntily in the most exposed place, so that the enemy should be under no misapprehension but that the outclassed little vessel would go down with her flag flying.

Some six weeks later, Nemesis, which had been on the track of the raider, caught her up in the shape of H.M.S. *Chatham*, which discovered the German hiding in the Rufiji River, opposite Mafia Island, in

German East Africa, later to be wrested from the *Kaiser* by the gallant South Africans under General Smuts.

The rest of the story reads like a romance from the pages of Marryat—with differences! The British officer in command of the operations sank a German liner in the mouth of the river, to prevent the raider from escaping, and then began shelling the cruiser. The *Königsberg*, however, managed to get out of range, and, in order more securely to bottle her up, a fairly large vessel, the collier *Newbridge*, was sent up river toward the island on which the German seamen had meantime entrenched themselves, with machine-guns and quick-firing guns for artillery. It was but poetic justice that Lieutenant Lavington, an officer who had been attached to the old *Pegasus*, should be placed in command of the *Newbridge* when she steamed up river on her hazardous mission. The collier was to be scuttled when she reached a position where her presence below the surface would effectually block the channel.

Lieutenant Lavington piloted his craft skilfully, and passing the fortified island, from which the entrenched Germans opened fire upon him, came to the appointed spot. The collier was then swung broadside across the channel and water was let into her port tank so that she took a list to stern, thus offering great resistance to the four-knot current running. This operation having been successfully achieved, the crew jumped for the steam launches which had followed in the wake of the *Newbridge* to take them back; buttons which connected electric wires with three charges of gun-cotton placed in the hold were pressed; there followed three terrific explosions, and the collier began to settle down to her last resting-place.

On the way back down river the gallant bluejackets had to run the gauntlet of the entrenched foe, who were using dum-dum bullets. There were a number of casualties, but the majority of the men succeeded in getting back unscathed to the waiting warships at the mouth of the river.

Although she was not disposed of until the following July, the *Königsberg's* days were numbered. To effect her final destruction elaborate preparations were made, but they were worthwhile. Two of the monitors, the *Severn* and the *Mersey*, which had been built for operations in shallow waters, were sent over to East Africa, together with a number of Royal Naval Air Service men and their machines. Headquarters were established at Mafia, from which place aerial observers went up to take notes of the exact position of the *Königsberg* in order that the monitors might be able to get the range.

To the man who knows nothing about atmospheric conditions and their effect upon aircraft, it may not seem a more hazardous venture to go up in East Africa than to do so in Western Europe, but the truth is that there is a vast difference. For instance, it is on record that a German aviator in South-west Africa could only fly over the Union camps at certain times of the day because of the effect of the heat upon his engine. And much the same conditions prevailed in East Africa, where, as the official account said:

> Most serious risks have been run by the officers and men who have flown in this climate, where the effect of the atmosphere and the extreme heat of the sun are quite unknown to those whose flying experience is limited to moderate climates. 'Bumps' of 250 feet have been experienced several times (which means that the aviator has dropped into an air-pocket, and slid down the emptiness so quickly that the effect of reaching normal conditions again, has given his machine an awful bump, in much the same way as a man jumping from a wall feels the jar when he hits the solid ground below), and the temperature varies from extreme cold, when flying at a great height, to a great heat, with burning tropical sun, when on land.

On April 25th, Flight-Commander Coll carried an observer from Mafia to where the *Königsberg* lay. It was only after considerable trouble that they located her, for she was hidden among the jungle, with tree trunks erected upon her decks to further conceal her. The Germans, who, it was supposed, had an observation and 'spotting' station at Pemba, were quickly apprised of the approach of the aeroplane, and her appearance was the signal for a heavy bombardment. Perhaps because the German gunners were not experienced in aerial shooting the machine was not brought down, but, as she had to descend to about 700 feet to enable the observer to take the required photographs, it is not to be wondered at that some shots got home, and that the engine of the aeroplane was badly damaged, although not so badly as to prevent the aviators returning to their base.

Final plans having been made, on July 6th Flight-Commander Harold E. M. Watkins, with Assistant-Paymaster Harold G. Badger of H.M.S. *Hyacinth*, (who had had no previous experience in flying, and had volunteered for the risky venture) as observer, left Mafia at 5.25 a.m., with a cargo of bombs, followed at 540 by Lieutenant-Commander Coll with Flight-Sub-Lieutenant H.J. Arnold as observer. The *Severn* and the *Mersey* were meantime moving up into the river, and while the monitors were taking up firing positions, and while Lieutenant Arnold was signalling his observations, the airmen in the first machine dropped their bombs, which action served to keep the Germans engaged. All being ready, the monitors opened fire, and at the same time H.M.S. *Weymouth* attended to Pemba observation station, with intent to distract the German gunners, that their bombardment at the monitors and also at the invaluable aeroplanes overhead might be ineffective.

The *Königsberg*, closely hidden in the dense jungle, was no easy mark, despite the aid of the aeroplanes, which, naturally, could not keep the air so long in those early days as is possible today. The result was that, although firing was opened at 6.30 a.m., by 12.35 little damage had been done to the *Königsberg*, chiefly because the aeroplanes, of which there were only two available, had continually to be relieving each other. The distance from the aerodrome to the site of the *Königsberg* was thirty miles, therefore "Considerable intervals elapsed between the departure of one and the arrival of its relief, and this resulted in loss of shooting efficiency." To make matters more difficult, just after half-past twelve one of the machines broke down, and the gunners on the monitors had to make the best they could of the one observer.

Naturally, the *Königsberg* was not taking her gruelling without a fight. Her gunners worked their guns well, and won praise from the admiral in charge of the British forces. The *Königsberg* replied, he wrote:

> Firing salvos of five guns with accuracy and rapidity. H.M.S. *Mersey* was hit twice, four men being killed and four wounded by one shell.

For six hours the bombardment had been going on, and the *Königsberg* was still intact, although she had been hit five times—not bad shooting, considering all the difficulties of 'spotting' the fall of the shots. Again the monitors fired a salvo, and the shells fell with devastating force upon her. The vessel was now seen to be heavily on fire between the masts. Then it was that the aeroplane broke down, and the work of observation was left to the second machine. The Germans had paid their respects also to the aviators, and many narrow escapes were experienced. But the work went on until 3.50, when the second machine was incapacitated for further work that day, and the operations came to a temporary close.

Although the *Königsberg* must by that time have been in an awful condition, her men were plucky, and she had continued to fire with one gun, intermittently, for some time after the fire had broken out. Eventually, however, she ceased firing, whether because her guns had all been put out of action or because ammunition had failed her was not known then. Certain it was that, if she were not entirely out of action, she was incapacitated, and would not give much trouble when the time came to put the finishing touches upon the work.

These final operations were carried out on July 11th, and Flight-Commander Coll, having got his machine in working order again, went out with Flight-Sub-Lieutenant Arnold, to 'spot' for the monitors, which had effected necessary repairs and taken in coal. The observation of Lieutenant Arnold was excellent, and it did not take long for the gunners on the monitors to get the exact range, whereupon they literally showered their explosives upon the doomed *Königsberg*, or what was left of her. Even then the Germans put up a good defence, trying to bring down the aeroplane, or else drive it away, and the aviators were in no little peril all the time. Eventually, when the work was almost completed, the Germans got home a shot which so badly damaged the machine that Lieutenant Arnold had to signal to the monitors that they were forced to descend and would try to land nearby.

From 3200 feet the aeroplane dropped to 2000 in a very short time, although Flight-Commander Coll did his best to keep up as long as possible. He knew that the work must be completed as quickly as possible, and that without his machine the gunners on the monitors would, to all intents and purposes, be helpless. His observer continued calmly to take note of each shot as it fell and to send back 'spotting' corrections. A quarter of an hour passed, the aeroplane dropping lower all the time, and the Germans making frantic efforts to finish their aerial enemy, until at last they succeeded in hitting it again, inflicting further injury, which made it imperative to go down at once. Even then, while the biplane maintained an even keel Lieutenant Arnold continued to send his 'spottings,' but at last flight was no longer possible. The machine, piloted very skilfully, came over the monitors, and then began to fall rapidly, turning over and over and finally plunging into the river near the *Mersey*, which, by the way, had been struck by shells from the *Königsberg*.

It was a dramatic moment. Flight-Commander Coll was entangled in the wreckage, so that he was in great peril. Lieutenant Arnold was able to disengage himself and with great gallantry went to his pilot's assistance. The soaked planes were dipping one after the other into the water, and the weight of the engine was gradually dragging the biplane down. Working feverishly yet systematically, at great risk to himself Lieutenant Arnold succeeded in extricating Coll from the wreckage. He was only just in time; a few more minutes and the pilot would have gone down with the wreck of the aeroplane on which he had done such good service.

Supporting his exhausted companion, Lieutenant Arnold awaited anxiously the arrival of a boat which he had seen set out from the *Mersey*. In a short time he and his burden were hauled into the craft, and taken on board the monitor, which, with her sister vessel, had meantime continued the bombardment of the helpless *Königsberg*. At 12.50 it was reported that the raider was on fire and would give no more trouble. The cruiser had not long survived the aeroplane!

It is evident that but for the good work done by the Royal Naval Air Service, the destruction of the *Königsberg* would have been far more difficult. In all probability a strong force of men would have had to have been landed, and they would have had to fight their way through the jungle and assault the entrenched Germans, an operation which would, no doubt, have been attended with considerable loss. The operations proved in a remarkable way the value of the newest arm in warfare.

CHAPTER 6

"One of Our Machines Did Not Return"

Behind the cold official announcements which tell only that "one of our machines has failed to return" there is, as may be supposed, very often a thrilling story, for several things, any one of which has possibilities and probabilities of dramatic character, may have happened to that machine.

Read, for instance, the story of Captain Thomas Chaloner, 13th Squadron, R.F.C., who, not having returned from a bombing raid on July 1st, 1916, was notified as "missing." Apparently a storm was brewing in the cauldron of the elements, but, as he wrote home, Captain Chaloner "did not see it," being engaged by a German at the time. Anxious to reach his objective rather than to try conclusions with a foe on the way, the captain set his engine going 'all out,' and succeeded in showing a mocking tail to the German. He was pursued, however, for some distance, and for a time his escape was not assured. To add to his perils he came within range of an anti-aircraft battery, over which he was flying, and only good handling and skilful steering got him out of that tight corner.

The captain was not yet out of the wood, however, for, he had hardly drawn clear when he became aware of another German machine about 200 feet above him. Again he put on his best speed, and as he drove along there came down to him the vicious snapping of a machine-gun. At first it did not occur to him that the German was attacking him! He wrote:

> I thought he was engaging another machine. When I looked up I saw that he and I were the only machines in sight, so I realized what was up.

As if to press home the seriousness of the situation, there came to the captain the sound of several sharp raps on his left plane, and looking in that direction, he saw three ominous little holes in the wing, which proved that the German was making good practice, and that it was necessary to take immediate action to deal with him. Captain Chaloner wasted no time; he stood his machine on its tail, and so bringing his gun in direct line with the hovering enemy, he emptied a whole drum into him. The German, however, roared past and over him, being enabled to do so with facility owing to the fact that his machine was probably twice as speedy as Captain Chaloner's. Before the Britisher could come about, his adversary had dropped behind and almost level with him, letting fly with his machine-gun as he did so. Chaloner replied with half a drum. Up went the German again, climbing with amazing rapidity, and coming right over the captain.

As he went he sprayed a few more rounds, and suddenly the captain's engine 'cut out,' and he knew that one of the bullets, at any rate, had found a sure billet, probably, so he guessed at the time, in his carburettor. Instantly the British machine began to glide, and the German, flying at a fair distance above, followed, expending occasional rounds as he did so. The situation was becoming unpleasant, and Captain Chaloner, although he knew that he was at a severe disadvantage, turned upon his foe and fired up at him, getting off about fifteen rounds. It was all very hopeless, however, for the British aeroplane, without a working engine, had absolutely no chance, and the pilot knew that he would be lucky if he reached *terra firma* alive. Suddenly his machine dived and then side-slipped, but the captain, cool-headed still, managed to regain control when he was within about 180 feet of the ground, and he finally glided safely to earth, to find himself surrounded by German infantry.

They carried him ten miles back toward the firing line—which shows that he had gone a considerable distance over the German lines—and after a while some German Flying Corps officers came up in a motorcar to claim him as their prize. The infantry opposed the claim, and there was a "lot of scrapping," as the captain wrote, but in the end the flying men won, and the prisoner was taken to their mess. There he met his antagonist, and also a number of British pilots who had been similarly unlucky. To the credit of the German flying men, let it be said that they treated Captain Chaloner well.

Behind the brief, laconic report issued of a raid on Schleswig-Holstein, on March 25th, 1916, there is a graphic tale of an air and sea attack, which was undertaken in circumstances which were very unfavourable and resulted, amongst other things, in certain airmen being reported as missing. When, over a twelvemonth before, our naval airmen had attacked Cuxhaven their efforts had not been so successful as they might have been because of a fog which hid the precious ships in harbour, and, similarly, the raid which we are about to describe had not the results which were expected of it owing to the inclement weather.

The expedition, consisting of light cruisers and destroyers and seaplanes, set out from its base at an hour which it was calculated would bring the force near to the German coast in the early morning. The evening was dark enough in all conscience, and as the ships held on their way the weather became very threatening, and at last they drove right into a howling blizzard. Commodore Tyrwhitt, who was in command of the expedition, knew that the trip to Germany was going to be no easy one; it would have been difficult even if only for the many minefields to be gone through, but with such a storm raging the dangers were increased tenfold.

One of those who took part in the affair told a *Scotsman* interviewer that:

> It was terrible work. The journey was long. It was not until one o'clock on Saturday morning that we got near the German coast. We were now going full steam ahead; all decks were cleared for action, the men standing by the guns, and the bows ploughed through the angry seas like razors. We managed to steer through the hidden dangers successfully, and about 3 a.m. the curtain went up on the strangest vision which has ever been seen in the North Sea.
> The weather quickly grew worse, and just as the show was about to begin a terrific gale sprang up! Battle-cruisers, destroyers and other craft were tossed about like corks. The wind was blowing fearfully, and more than once we were in such a plight that many of us yelled 'Goodbye, England, home, and beauty!' To make matters worse a terrific snowstorm came on, and the North Sea seemed to undergo a complete transformation. Nothing looked more unlikely than a battle in such weather conditions.

And indeed those same weather conditions caused the seaplane raid to be postponed for a while. Apparently the German fleet was not keen on coming out to give battle, and as their ships lolloped off the coast, the British seamen whiled away the time with gramophones, the favourite record on that dark and dismal morn being, "Here we are, here we are again!"—an invitation to the enemy to join issue. The commodore, realizing that the weather was not likely to change, eventually decided to let loose his falcons, five of which were sent up in the teeth of the driving storm.

We will leave the story of those seaplanes for a while in order to tell of what happened to their escort during the time the bombers were winging their way toward the airship sheds on the island of Sylt. The German patrol boats, in due course, came within striking distance of the British vessels, and simultaneously both sides opened fire through the blizzard. The snow was falling so densely, however, that it was difficult to retain any organized formation, and the action developed into a series of isolated duels. The British ships lost no opportunity of punishing their opponents, who were chased relentlessly whenever they were sighted through the snow. Two armed trawlers felt the weight and the smother of British gun-fire and gave no further trouble. British destroyers were quickly at work picking up struggling survivors, but the work of rescue was not easy, and danger lurked behind the snow-bank.

The dense veil of snow baffled all efforts on the part of lookout men, and it happened that the *Medusa* suddenly found herself face to face, as it were, with one of her consorts. The discovery was made too late to avoid collision, and with a rending crash the two ships swept into each other, the *Medusa* getting the worst of the encounter. On the instant it was "Out boats!" on the other destroyers, and while at several points of the far-reaching scene of battle, guns were roaring, yellow-red flashes were rending the darkness, and shells were screaming through the air, stirring deeds were being enacted in the effort to save as many as possible of the Medusa's men, some of whom were in the water, while others were being transferred from their doomed vessel before she went down.

Both fleets used the same tactics for different purposes: the Germans sought to lure the British ships on to the minefields nearer the coast, while the British vessels tried to coax the Germans out to sea by offering themselves as bait. From the "dashing in" tactics which they had first used the Britons fell back to what seemed to be flight; they suddenly "swooped round," said one who was present, "to give the enemy the impression that we were beating a hasty retreat." The *ruse de guerre* was successful; German cruisers and torpedo-boat destroyers, confident that they now had their enemy on the run and possibly at their mercy, swept out to the chase, which lasted just as long as the British desired it to. They then swung round as one ship and bombarded the disillusioned Germans with all the guns they could bring to bear.

Despite the awful weather conditions the British gunners got in some fine shots, as was evident when, the snow occasionally clearing, enemy destroyers were seen to be blazing from end to end. The last that was seen of two of them showed that they were in that fiery plight, and in view of the heavy weather it is not a little doubtful whether they could have reached the port for which they and their consorts were hastening with the British shells dropping like a hurricane at their heels.

Yet one other German destroyer met her doom during that terrific fight by the little-used method of modern naval warfare, the ram. H.M.S. *Cleopatra*, cutting through the seas with well-nigh the highest power of her engines, her bows hidden from sight by the huge waves she created, suddenly came through the snow upon a German destroyer. The unlucky boat had never experienced such a hurricane of fire as was poured upon her as the *Cleopatra* came rapidly up. The light cruiser headed directly for the enemy, who tried in vain to turn off the approaching foe by her gunfire. Probably the time was too short to allow of a torpedo being launched, but the risk was great, and the British commander took a desperate and determined resolve. His action was reminiscent of the olden days, and the Germans must have been wholly unprepared for the stroke.

Throbbing with the full energy of her powerful engines, the *Cleopatra* drove straight for her victim and her sharp bows bit deeply into the steel hull of the German. The awful impact shook the cruiser from bow to stern and made even her own strong-hearted crew wonder whether their ship would survive. But the British cruiser was little damaged, and the destroyer, listing heavily, with the sea pouring into the great rent in her hull, fell away, to be hidden immediately by another curtain of snow which fell at that moment.

The sea affair had ended successfully and the British crews were highly pleased with their work. But what of the airmen?

The leader of the raiders was Flight-Lieutenant G. H. Reid, and of the band of Naval Air Service men who went on that bombing expedition five, including Lieutenant Reid himself, Flight-Sub-Lieutenant

J. F. Hay, Chief Petty Officer Mullins, and two others, failed to return.

The trip out to the airship sheds was uneventful, but when the naval men came within sight of their objective it was clear that they were to experience a warm reception. Anti-aircraft batteries barked angrily and the air was filled with screaming shells and whistling bullets, but the aviators sailed courageously on their way, and as each passed over the long lines which he knew to be sheds, he loosed his bombs, drove on, and then swept round in a circle which led him out seaward. It was a strenuous and dangerous business, for the driving snowstorm lashed the machines, and the snow coated the glass of the airmen's goggles and blinded them. The German gunners, too, were making good practice; such good practice, indeed, that two machines were brought down. One of these, a small mount carrying Sub-Lieutenant Hay, tumbled into the sea just off the coast.

Among the rest. Lieutenant Reid, leader of the raiders, was fighting his way through the snowstorm, shells bursting above and below and around him, so that he seemed to be encircled by a ring of explosions. Safety lay in putting as great a distance as possible, in as short a time as possible, between himself and the batteries below, but looking down, the lieutenant was startled to see a seaplane drifting on the water, buffeted by the wind and waves, and the figure of a man struggling beside it.

Lieutenant Reid recognized that the wrecked machine was the single-seater which had carried Lieutenant Hay, and although he might have succeeded in getting away had he pushed on, the gallant airman planed down through the crashing shells, alighted on the water, and taxied toward the now almost submerged seaplane, which was presently reached. A heavy sea was running and Reid and his mechanic had to use all their skill and cunning to keep their machine steady and at the same time hold on to the almost exhausted sub-lieutenant. Despite all the difficulties, however, and regardless of the fact that the Germans were continually firing heavily at them, Lieutenant Reid and his mechanic, C. P. O. Mullins, at last managed to drag the wrecked aviator into the body of their machine, where they fixed him up as comfortably as was possible. He was chilled to the bone, and almost unconscious by reason of his exposure and the drenching he had received.

It was now time to attend again to their own safety. Lieutenant Reid opened out his engine and set the seaplane taxiing along the rough waters, expecting it to rise in due course. The machine, however, refused to do anything of the kind, and the pilot could neither coax it nor force it. Nothing but the purr of the engine and a short, sharp spurt followed his efforts.

And alas! Lieutenant Reid could see a German ship ploughing its way through the heaving seas. Steadily forward the vessel came, and the sight of her made the airman redouble his efforts to get up and away. The wind seemed to force his machine downward every time he thought he had it on the rise; the water seemed to be clinging to the floats and refusing to let go. It was maddening!

It is easy to imagine what thoughts were running through the minds of the three Britons as they sat in their obstinate mount: to rise and wing out across the sea meant freedom and opportunity to fight again; to stay there, until that forging ship reached them, meant captivity until the world-war was over! Never did men work more determinedly than they; but weather and water were against them; they lay rocking helplessly on the surface, and knew at last that they were doomed.

When the German ship came up there was nothing for it but to submit with the best possible grace, and the shivering, drenched, wretched-looking three were hauled aboard, to be consigned to a prison camp and enforced idleness for many a long day to come.

Sometimes news of what happens to those who are posted 'missing' comes, not through letters received from the men themselves, but from neutral correspondents with the German army. In such cases the censor sees to it that the narrator does not tell too much, but there is one story at least which filtered through to America of a battle royal in which British aviators were worsted.

On a cloudless September day, in 1916, spectators at the German Headquarters in Picardy saw four tiny specks appear in the sky. The setting sun provided an appropriate background for what was about to be enacted. Evidently hostile aeroplanes were approaching, for puffs of bursting shrapnel from the anti-aircraft guns began to play about the points of black. Those shells seemed to be very near to the oncoming aeroplanes, although it afterward transpired that they were falling nearly a mile short of the nearest machine. The specks grew larger, the guns roared continuously, and the watchers presently saw a couple of German machines rise swiftly behind the raiders as though to cut them off.

Everyone was now on the *qui vive*, waiting for the combat to begin. It was clear that the visitors were British, yet there was not one of the lookers-on who did not admire the way in which the four pilots sailed over the gun positions, apparently quite untroubled by the bursts of shrapnel.

Presently it became evident that one of the raiders had caught sight of one of the German machines, for he began to dive.

But it is time for us to see what was happening in that British biplane, and we have available the report of the newspaper correspondent who interviewed the pilot and observer afterward.

Lieutenant Douglas Stewart, the observer, sweeping the limitless space with his binoculars, had spotted one of those uprising German aeroplanes, and, informing his pilot, Captain A. S. Salmond, prepared for the moment when Captain Salmond should decide to attack. The Lewis guns were unshipped and ready when the biplane turned in her course and dived steeply. The cross-marked wings grew rapidly larger and Briton and German met in mortal combat 8000 feet up. Unhappily for Captain Salmond and his observer, their attention was taken up by their one foe, and they did not see that a second hawk was on their trail.

The British machine, which had dropped about 2500 feet, engaged the first enemy at some 600 yards, and there followed a sharp exchange of about a dozen rounds of ammunition without much harm being caused to either combatant.

And then came disaster for the Britons.

The second German 'plane, which had succeeded in getting well over the British craft, suddenly poured in a stream of bullets. One plugged into Stewart's cheek, another cut the collar of his tunic to rags and narrowly missed his throat, while a third scraped the pilot's face. Stewart was flung off his seat on to the floor of the nacelle, and was badly bruised. He had sufficient strength to ram another drum into his gun, and, determined to make a good show, he emptied this at the enemy, although he could not get back into his seat, and had to fire lying down.

He realized, in that moment when the machine was swaying frightfully, that there was little chance for him and his companion. "It was a pretty fight," he said, "but fate was against us." Fate indeed was against them, for the German's hurricane of bullets crackled all over the machine, and presently the pilot's control was carried away. It was now impossible to get out of the tight corner and the British machine was utterly at the mercy of the foe, whose shots now cut away the struts of one of the wings, which immediately collapsed.

A British aeroplane ablaze after a duel with a giant biplane

Like a bird with broken wing, the doomed aeroplane dropped at lightning speed, followed by the victor. Seven thousand five hundred feet Captain Salmond saw that his altimeter was registering, and he knew that there was little likelihood, unless a miracle happened, of either he or his observer escaping with life. Grim, silent, facing death, those two intrepid men sat in their nacelle, the pilot doing all he could with his smashed controlling gear to prevent the machine from turning too many of those fearful somersaults which so often have resulted in death.

The splendid skill and nerve of Captain Salmond triumphed, the tragedy was obviated, and when the machine reached earth, the two men, although badly shaken and sorely battered, were still alive—indeed, they had no bones broken!

In the spirit of *camaraderie* which seems especially to distinguish the men of the rival flying services, the German victors, it is pleasant to add, treated their prisoners courteously while they were at the flying base.

We will conclude this chapter with one other story told by a newspaper correspondent with the German army.

One day during September 1916, Captain Boelcke,[1] the man who competed with Immelmann for the reputation of being champion flying fighter of Germany, attacked Captain R. E. Wilson of the R.F.C., and after some excellent fighting on the part of both succeeded in holing Captain Wilson's tank.

The petrol flowed over the machine, and instantly there was a tremendous blaze which enveloped the whole aeroplane. Knowing that if he would save his life he must descend at once, Captain Wilson immediately sent his machine diving for earth. It needs grit to keep one's seat with the flames roaring around as the machine slips through the air. Captain Wilson was badly burned, and any man could be excused who in a moment of such agony as the airman must have suffered lost his head and leapt out of his machine.

But Captain Wilson kept his head, maintained perfect control over his mount, and actually succeeded in bringing it to rest as gracefully as he would have done in normal circumstances, much to the astonishment of the Germans, who had expected to see the machine crash heavily to earth, the flaming bier of its pilot.

---

1. *Richthofen & Böelcke in Their Own Words* by Manfred Freiherr von Richthofen (*The Red Battle Flyer*) & Oswald Böelcke (*An Aviator's Field Book*) also published by Leonaur.

CHAPTER 7

First-Aid in Midair

The manner in which Sub-Lieutenant Oxley won his D.S.C. reveals an amazing degree of coolness and audacity—those two distinguishing qualities of British airmen.

King Fox of Bulgaria and his brood, when they entered the arena of the European War, probably did not realize that far-off Britain would send her aerial fighters over their cities; but the men of the Royal Naval Air Service might certainly take *Ubique!* as their motto.

Choosing the most opportune moment, Bulgaria 'came in' and, pouncing upon the back of gallant Serbia, helped to smash her; and so our naval airmen did what they could to take toll of the Bulgars for their treachery. Day after day the coast of the traitor-kingdom was raided, and bombs fell with destructive effect upon places of military importance; and not all the efforts of the enemy could keep off the gallant airmen of Britain. Not merely in ones and twos, but in whole squadrons the fliers went, spreading terror wherever they appeared.

When Sub-Lieutenant Oxley, flying as observer in a battle-plane piloted by Flight-Lieutenant Dunning, D.S.C., won his Cross, he was on escort and reconnaissance patrol for a flight of bombing machines the objective of which lay "somewhere on the Bulgarian coast." As it happened, the day, June 20th, 1916, was as fine a day as could be wished either for a flight or a fight.

The battle-plane, as distinct from the bomb- droppers, hummed on steadily in advance, ready to engage any enemy craft bold enough to attack; and Oxley was busy all the time not merely in looking out for hovering foemen, but in taking observations of the countryside. After a while, his attention was distracted from note-taking by the sudden appearance of two machines, approaching from inland. The pilot, Lieutenant Dunning, knew that these would prove to be enemies, and eagerly made toward them, driving into as close range as was possible; and then a fierce fight began. Both enemy machines took part, trying to bring down their intrepid opponent, who, however, darted hither and thither, soared up and over this foe, swooped down and under the other, incessantly endeavouring to outmanoeuvre them. While Dunning steered his machine skilfully, striving ever to secure the most advantageous position, Oxley worked the machine-gun, giving one enemy the benefit of a drum full of cartridges, and then slipping in another as Dunning swooped toward the foe who was attacking from another point.

Quick work—a thrilling game—a gamble with the death that might come before the next revolution of the propeller! Battles in the air do not, as a rule, last long, though a whole eternity of experience may seem to be crammed into the few minutes between attack and retreat—or disaster. Oxley and Dunning passed through all the stages of such combats: advance to attack, engagement, circling round their foes, mounting higher and then dropping lower, giving shots and receiving shots, never able to efface the subconscious thought that they might be doomed to that swift destruction which is so often the airman's end; and when Dunning felt a sudden burning pain in his left leg, and there was the thump of bullets as they entered the petrol tank, it seemed that the climax had come. Dunning set his teeth, Oxley trained his gun at the nearest foe: they would die fighting anyway.

But, there was no need to die! The enemy, not realizing that they had wounded both pilot and machine, and having themselves had quite sufficient drubbing for one day, suddenly turned tail and drummed off in retreat!

As soon as he saw that Dunning was injured. Lieutenant Oxley got to work. The home aerodrome was a good way off, and Dunning might bleed to death if his wound was not stopped, so Oxley improvised a tourniquet, which he contrived to pass over to his disabled companion with a scribbled note telling him to fix it on his leg and to relinquish control of the machine so that he himself might take charge.

Then, while the aeroplane was spinning through the air, Oxley scrambled over from his own seat into that occupied by the pilot, the latter shifted, Oxley took his place, and, while Dunning applied the tourniquet to the pumping wound in his leg, the observer steered the racing machine toward their base. Dunning made himself as comfortable as possible, and then turned his attention to the injured petrol tank. It was leaking badly, and unless the leak were stopped the machine would have to descend a long way from home. The pilot solved the problem in the most primitive way: he simply kept his thumb over the hole, and in this way succeeded in preventing fuel from escaping, except when, because of the strain on his hand, it became absolutely necessary to change thumbs!

Such was the manner of the home-coming; and the aeroplane, although bearing numerous signs of her dramatic encounter, in the shape of riddled planes, dented fuselage, penetrated tank, and what not, glided gracefully down to earth, making an excellent landing.

A scarcely less remarkable instance of first-aid during an aerial battle is that in which Captain A. E. Borton (Black Watch and R.F.C.) was the wounded pilot, and Captain Anthony Marshall (28th Light Cavalry, Indian Army, and R.F.C.) was the observer, both of whom eventually received the D.S.O., in "recognition of their gallantry and devotion to duty." The aviators were on an important reconnaissance flight in the neighbourhood of Staden, on June 7th, 1915, when they were attacked by a hostile aeroplane. In the course of the combat the enemy gunner succeeded in getting home a bullet which severely wounded Captain Borton in the neck and head. The result was that the captain began to bleed most profusely, and it was clear that unless something was at once done for him he would become unconscious. There was no time to return to the base, despite the fact that the machine was a fast one, for the aviators were faced by the all-important fact that it was vitally necessary for the reconnaissance to be carried to completion.

Somewhere behind the lines a red-collared staff officer was waiting anxiously for the report. Captain Marshall, by the blood reddening the aviator's coat and the way in which the pilot himself was sagging in his seat, soon realized the seriousness of his comrade's wounds, and he speedily improvised bandages with which he and the pilot himself, while the machine was still pelting through the air under strict control—amazing achievement!—succeeded in temporarily binding up the wound and somewhat stanching the flow of blood. That done, Captain Borton steered his machine over the course which had been mapped out for the reconnaissance. The enemy aeroplane, which had persistently been attacking all the time that first-aid was in progress, now followed after them, its pilot's intention being to drive them back and so prevent them from making their observations.

Captain Borton, gallantly summoning all his reserves of strength and keeping his head as cool as man can under such circumstances, bravely piloted his machine, though every moment was filled with agony for him and brought nearer and nearer a state of unconsciousness. Incredible though it sounds, not only was the persistent enemy kept at a distance, but Captain Marshall, in between times of rattling out drums of cartridges at the foe, was also busy taking most valuable notes.

As the German swooped to attack, Captain Borton banked and turned, dived or rose as the exigencies of the attack demanded, although concentration of mind was difficult. It was a perfect whirl of manoeuvring and out-manoeuvring, and yet through it all the notebook was being entered up; until at last, having done all that which they had been sent out to do, the two gallant aviators bethought them of the home station, banked suddenly and swung round, to the momentary bewilderment of their antagonist, and then, with their engine all out, sped up and on. Each second now was precious, for it was clear to Captain Marshall that his companion was in sorry plight and might at any instant crumple up in his seat, lose control, and let the aeroplane go spinning earthward. However, by a mighty effort, Captain Borton fought the insidious desire to let go of all things, kept his controls working almost mechanically, and succeeded in making a safe landing. Captain Marshall, immediately he had seen his comrade lifted from the machine, made his report, which, so the official record put it, "was as detailed and complete for the last as it was for the first part of the reconnaissance."

Pluck? Determination? Yes! *Verily of such stuff are the kings of the air made!*

CHAPTER 8

Warneford, V.C.

In the year 1892, there was born in the Indian city of Cooch-Behar an English boy named Warneford, who was destined some twenty years later to become one of the heroes of our Empire. As he grew to manhood, this boy was fascinated with the new science of flight, and shortly after the great European War had begun he was able to obtain a commission in the Royal Naval Air Service, being posted for training at the Hendon Aerodrome. Here he obtained his 'ticket' in February 1915. Later, he went overseas, and was one of those brilliant pilots who quickly made names for themselves by their raids into the territory occupied by the enemy.

Very early on the morning of June 7th, 1915, Lieutenant Warneford and two brother officers, Flight-Lieutenants Wilson and Mills, went up from their station "somewhere in Flanders," bound for the big Zeppelin hangars at Evere, a few miles to the north of Brussels. Aloft, the early morning was very misty, but steering chiefly by compass the three pilots made direct for their objective. As they flew, the slight haze cleared and in due course the Belgian capital could be seen spread out below. The gigantic airship sheds of the Evere aerodrome could also be discerned, and accordingly the machines piloted by Wilson and Mills turned to attack, whilst Warneford, making away to the north, came round in a gigantic circle, an aerial spectator of his comrades' attempts on the sheds.

Wilson and Mills were by this time gliding lower and lower, and their machines being now visible from the ground the German anti-aircraft batteries guarding the sheds were getting to work. Quite suddenly. Mills put the nose of his bus down and swooped at the hangar. He was soon temporarily out of danger from the 'Archibald' shells, but within range of rifle fire, which was at once opened upon him.

He could see the nose of a Zeppelin protruding from the hangar, so he knew that if he succeeded in hitting the shed he would most certainly destroy the dirigible inside. At an altitude of not more than five hundred feet he dropped three of his bombs in rapid succession. One of these missiles went through the roof of the hangar as if it had been cardboard and, bursting, ripped the top of the envelope of the airship inside.

As the hydrogen from the torn ballonets rushed out and mixed with the air, it was immediately set on fire by the burning outer fabric, with the result that the airship and shed instantly became a roaring furnace. The hundreds of Belgians who had climbed to the tops of their houses to view the affair saw clearly a pillar of flame over 200 feet in height rise into the still morning air, and forgetting the fact that the Hun ruled them with a rod of iron, gave vent to a roar of cheers.

Meanwhile, Wilson and Mills on their fast little mounts were climbing aloft as rapidly as their engines would drive them; and, except for a few bullet holes in the planes of Mills' machine, both winged their way back toward their own base none the worse for their adventure.

Warneford, observing that his comrades had effectively 'strafed' their Zeppelin, made away on a private tour of his own, hoping for something to turn up.

The Fates were kind to him, and about three o'clock, when the early sun was driving the last of the night mists from the sky, he sighted in the far distance a long grey shape. Hardly believing his own eyes, he flew nearer, and convinced himself that ahead there was indeed one of Count Zeppelin's gigantic creations on the wing. He immediately tilted his elevators, and the sensitive little mono-plane in which he was flying at once commenced to cause the needle of his altimeter to tremble along the feet. In those early days it was only possible to 'strafe' a gas-bag by getting above it, and he knew that it was imperative that he should be well above the monster before he commenced to attack. The 80-horse-power Gnome had gallantly set him at a splendid altitude before the men in the cars of the Zeppelin discovered the small speck in the sky that spelled terrible danger to themselves. They at once went ahead at full speed, and tilting their elevators and letting go some of their water-ballast attempted to rise to the same level as their antagonist and there keep him at bay—by means of the machine-guns mounted in the gondolas.

Warneford at once noted the movement of his gigantic antagonist and decided to attack before the Zeppelin, which he knew could climb even faster than his own little mount, outmanoeuvred him.

But though he wished to drive in upon his quarry, the latter doubled away and he was compelled to chase the monster for some time. Having the heels of her, he was fortunately able to climb as he chased, and at the same time gain steadily upon his enemy. When the Zeppelin had reached an altitude of 6000 feet she temporarily stopped climbing, and it was at this juncture that Warneford swooped down upon her. The speed indicator moved higher and higher until the terrific speed of 110 miles an hour was being recorded, and still he dived toward the broad back of the airship. He could not hear the crackle of the enemy machine-guns, but it is certain that they were firing at him all this time, though he presented an almost impossible target.

At last he was directly above the dirigible, and the observer on top must have screamed some awful messages into his telephone in those last few minutes of his life. It must have been apparent to this man that the mad Englishman intended to ram them and send all to 'glory' together, for the undercarriage was little more than twenty yards above the top of the Zeppelin when Warneford flattened out and let go his bombs. At this range it was almost impossible to miss, and in fact he dropped three bombs, all of which took effect. In an instant, as it seemed, the huge envelope was a sheet of flame. Then a tremendous explosion shook the air.

Although Warneford had quickly banked away to get clear, the flames from his victim singed him; then the great up-rush of air from the doomed airship caught his swaying little mount and tossed him upward as though the machine were in the grip of a tornado, causing Warneford to make an involuntary 'loop.' She then put her nose down and, with the dazed pilot still strapped in his seat, commenced to rush headlong for the ground. At this second the young pilot regained control of himself, and in a few moments had also resumed command of his mount. His Gnome was back-firing and missing, which gave him a pretty sure indication that something was wrong with his petrol supply. How could matters be righted?

Warneford made up his mind to go down and attempt to rectify things before any of his enemies could capture him. He selected a fairly deserted piece of country, alighted, and, even as he stopped, he was out of his seat and round to the Gnome. Once more he was back peering into the fuselage, for oil was running down, which meant a bad leakage of petrol. Quickly he noted which of the two tanks that he carried was leaking, emptied its remaining fuel into the other tank, reconnected the feed-pipe to the carburettor, then leaped into his seat again. This work had taken him nearly thirty-five minutes, and already he could observe German troops coming across the fields, firing as they ran.

These were moments pregnant with excitement for Warneford. If his engine 'fired' he would be up and away well before the enemy reached him, but if it refused to start there was nothing for him but a German prison—at the best. At his command a Belgian peasant swung his propeller for him, and at once the Gnome started into a healthy roar. Then opening her out he went bouncing along the ground, and with a steady rush soared aloft toward the sea and safety. Behind him the blazing wreckage of his victim had fallen upon the convent buildings of St Elizabeth, which had also caught fire, and a great coil of black smoke was rising into the morning sky.

Warneford soon sighted the sea, and making along the coast espied Cape Gris-Nez, where he landed, and shortly afterward the news was sent out far and wide telling the story of this first successful fight with a Zeppelin in midair. Warneford's name was in everybody's mouth, and after the Legion of Honour had been bestowed upon him by our gallant Allies, he was received by King George, who personally pinned the Victoria Cross upon his blue tunic. News which filtered through revealed the consternation of the Germans over the loss of the great gas-bag. Strangely perturbed, too, were the Zeppelin-builders, and the reason for this was that the destroyed dirigible had not only contained a picked crew, but also carried a number of experts from the factory, who were making the trip for experimental purposes; and though other gas-bags could be built and other crews trained, it was practically impossible to replace quickly the expert brains which had also perished.

Unfortunately, the gallant Warneford did not live long to enjoy his well-earned honours. Ten days after his great and successful duel he was in Paris and went aloft in a machine that was just as stable and easy to control as his own Morane-Saulnier 'Parasol' was difficult. With him, as passenger, was an American journalist. When they were at a few hundred feet, the machine was seen to nosedive, and, owing to the fact that Warneford had no space to pull her out, the big bus crashed to the ground and was wrecked, killing instantly both pilot and passenger.

The end of the hero came as a great shock to the world, but his name will ever be remembered as the man who, unaided by the devices that were later used by airmen to bring down dirigibles, was the first to attack and successfully destroy a Zeppelin in the air.

CHAPTER 9

Flying While Dying

There is a story told of two French airmen who, while on a reconnaissance, met with disaster in midair—a tragic mishap whereby the pilot was robbed of his sight and the observer was mortally wounded; and yet both returned to headquarters with their information. The dying observer gave directions to the blinded pilot, telling him when to fly high and when to fly low, and thus, followed by bursting shrapnel, the heroes got their machine home.

We are concerned only with British airmen, however, so we may not do more than mention that grim story—perhaps one of the grimmest of the war, certainly one of the most heroic; but the flying men of Britain also number among their heroes who have 'gone west' men who similarly finished their flights racing against certain death.

Such a one, for instance, was Lieutenant Rhodes-Moorhouse.

An order came to this young officer to bomb the vital railway junction at Courtrai. This was a task after his own heart, for besides being exceedingly dangerous, it would, if successful, disorganize the enemy's communications. Through Courtrai German troop trains continually bore reinforcements to Ypres—that long-held, blood-consecrated salient of the British line in Flanders. The destruction of the station, the tearing up of yards of the steel road, would effectively hinder the flow of these reinforcements, as Rhodes-Moorhouse knew. He knew, also, that there were anti-aircraft guns everywhere, for the Germans realized that important junctions must attract British airmen, and a warm reception awaited the man who would dare to come humming overhead.

Such risks, however, are as the spice of life to the flying man, and the lieutenant mounted to his seat, waved *au revoir* to his comrades at the air station, and alone, on that April 27th, 1915, guided his rapid biplane over the German lines, potted at here and there by 'Archibalds,' but holding jauntily on his way. Soon it seemed that every anti-aircraft gun within range was in action; shrapnel puffs hung around the intrepid flier like balls of wool, and bullets whistled all about him. And these came not only from the shells, for innumerable rifles blazed from the trenches; every German grey-coat within shooting distance let fly—and rifle bullets are by no means to be despised by the airman, since they can pierce a petrol tank, or smash a delicate steering gear, to say nothing of finding a mark in the pilot's body.

But the gods of the air and of brave men seemed to be watching over the gallant aviator, for he escaped all injury, and succeeded in making many valuable observations of the German positions and their strength. Though keeping at a good height he was flying not too high to see that which he was out to see.

Courtrai at last lay beneath him—Courtrai with its fussing trains, its thousands of cannon-fodder ready for the inferno of the front lines, Courtrai with its massed anti-aircraft guns. The town looked a fine mark for bombs, but Rhodes-Moorhouse knew from past experience that there is little certainty of hitting any mark when one is many thousands of feet above the ground. He also knew well enough that there is no little risk in coming down low enough to be sure of doing it. But, the mark had to be hit, those were the orders, and without stopping to calculate chances he 'planed down from his height of comparative safety, and with the precision acquired by the cool-headed, practised airman, came to within 300 feet of the railway junction.

Three hundred feet! Think of it! Not so high above the ground as is the golden cross of St Paul's Cathedral. And within range—easy range—of the rifle of every German there, to say nothing of the 'Archibalds!'

As the machine ceased volplaning and righted itself, gliding upon an even keel, as it were, every rifleman blazed away, every anti-aircraft gun spat fire; bullets sped upward through the fabric of the planes, and whistled their tunes of death in the airman's ears. And then came new sounds—the explosion of bombs dropped in quick succession as Rhodes-Moorhouse released them from their gear. Holes yawned in the ground, the steel lines of the railway were wrenched from their ties, and the junction presented a scene of woeful destruction. Men scattered in all directions as the balls of death came hurtling through the air; but some stuck to their posts and bullets continued to whistle about the lieutenant. Suddenly one struck him in the thigh with a sickening thud that told him it was no light wound he had received. Soon his garments were wet with his blood and he realized that probably the only way to save his life was to go down at once and surrender to the Germans.

Rhodes-Moorhouse gritted his teeth: away back at the flying base were officers waiting for his report, and if the god of good luck would have it so, they should get that for which they waited. All the bombs were gone now, and the biplane swept on its way. Suddenly it banked, so steeply that the foes beneath thought that the airman was about to come tumbling in their midst. They did not know Rhodes-Moorhouse. Instead of falling, he turned an amazing circle, and, in order to get up top speed, rushed downward to within a hundred feet of the hard-working gunners and riflemen. Then—up, and up— rising from the depths of danger to the heights of safety, he headed swiftly for the base. Realizing that the prey they had thought certain was escaping, the Germans increased the intensity and rapidity of their fire. The Englishman seemed to be flying in a cloud of shrapnel; it would be remarkable if he escaped further injury. He did not escape: once again that stinging, burning pain, and the shock of it made him all but lose control. A momentary gasp, a brief haze before the eyes, a quick pulling of himself together—and his now clearer mind told him the truth: he was wounded to the death.

The base—the men waiting at the base for his return: that thought alone sustained him. The biplane answered his slightest touch and seemed to leap upward in bounds away from the drumming bullets and the sharp crack of the bursting shrapnel. At top speed he went, for it was to be a race to reach home before death for ever silenced him. He was still over the German lines, but he swept on past them, across No Man's Land and over the British front line. Even then he did not go down to get the medical aid he so sorely needed: at the base only must he stop.

He now commenced to drop from the giddy altitude, still driving his machine at full speed, until coming at last within sight of the flying base he shut off his engine, set his machine at a decline, and, cool as a man in the full flush of life, though his body was numb with coming death and a mist was before his eyes, volplaned to a perfect landing.

Men rushed to his assistance, not knowing how sorely he needed it, nor yet how useless their help, save to get him out of the winged chariot of death. But they knew when they saw his face and lifted his limp body from the seat....

He made his report calmly, like a soldier who has done unscathed what he went to do; men accustomed to coolness marvelled at him as they carried him to hospital.

He died, and in his death, as "Eyewitness" wrote, the nation lost "a very gallant life." Could any man have a better, nobler epitaph?

CHAPTER 10

Rescued by Airmen

To say that a roaring aeroplane swooped down through the air, landed, and in the presence of a host of running foes waited for a stranded man to straddle across its fuselage and then pounded back into the sky with its salvage, is to lay oneself open to the charge of being melodramatic. But it nevertheless is sober fact that on more than one occasion during the war an intrepid pilot, flying at a great height, having seen a comrade's machine go crashing earthward, has dived after him, intent upon giving what aid might be possible, realizing that if the unfortunate pilot escaped more than likely death he would be taken prisoner.

High up in the clear blue sky skimmed the glittering dot which friend and foe alike knew to be an aeroplane, and, because it came from seaward, recognized it as a British machine out on a reconnaissance and, maybe, on a bombing expedition. Far out to sea grim grey outlines belched fire and smoke—and away behind the hills, that seemed like impregnable barriers to victorious progress, the earth went up in miniature eruptions; while from gun-pits hidden on the shelving beach, or in amongst the ravines which had been won in many a sanguinary battle, the 'heavies' of the Anzacs hurled their little less destructive high explosives at the enemy hidden in cunningly devised dugouts on hillside and in gulch.

And the aviator—it was Flight-Sub-Lieutenant Smylie, R.N.A.S., speeding inland—was out to bomb the railway station, Ferrijik Junction. The shimmering planes caught the sunlight and gleamed like points of gold; white puffs of smoke broke out all around, yet although the covering of the planes was riddled by the shrapnel, the Royal Naval Air Service man held on. Nerves of steel, head clear as age-old wine, every faculty alert, he was picking up this tit-bit of information, that seeming anthill with swarms of ants which none but an observer from above could discover; and he cared nothing for the 'Archibalds,' except that they might—who could tell?—send him hurtling below, in which case General Headquarters would never know what he had found out.

And then, when the work was almost done, came the climax: an ominous silence—then the thunder again—then once more silence, and so on. The airman knew what had happened—his engine was playing him false! There is a vast difference between being 'pinked' by a foe and being treated scurvily by your own machine; and the man in the single-seater biplane soaring so gaily a moment before over the hills of Gallipoli said strong things about the engine which in calmer moments he had often lovingly tended.

You cannot repair a fault in an engine when you are in midair, although, if you know how, you can do miracles of many kinds with aeroplanes while they are on the wing. In this present instance it was a case of going down to see what was wrong and trying to put it right. So Lieutenant Smylie put his machine at an angle and went volplaning down the giddy depths of air, taking the man-bird's chance that he might land in a lonely place.

One thing consoled him in his wrath, and that was that he had disposed, usefully, as far as he could make out, of all his bombs but one; and Ferrijik Junction was smoking and blazing as a result. He snapped his teeth together grimly as he thought of the luck that was really his after all in having that one left—it would come in handy later, perhaps.

The biplane glided down like a swallow, the earth seemed to be rising up to meet it; an amateur sitting in the fuselage would have felt his heart stop with the fear of the coming crash. But, instead, there was a slight jar, a rebound, and another jar slighter than ever; then stillness except for the quivering twang of the planes. Quickly unstrapping himself, the airman stepped out, slipped his goggles over on to his forehead and began to inspect the engine which had brought him down, as he realized, in the enemy's territory. What, however, he did not know at that moment was that a party of Turks had seen the volplaning machine, and, judging the spot where it would land, were rushing toward it, hugely delighted at the prospect of their prize.

The lieutenant tinkering away at his engine, having discovered the secret of its awkwardness, suddenly straightened his bent back. Two things he had heard—the rushing of feet behind him and the hum of something above. Quickly looking round, he saw a number of Turks pelting along the rough ground, so near that he could see the grins of victory on their dirty faces.

"No need to try to tinker the old thing now," he muttered to himself, and made a leap away from the aeroplane, after having set fire to his machine, knowing that this would explode the bomb and so ensure the destruction of the aeroplane. At the same time he looked up.

What he saw set his blood a-tingling—a single-seater biplane similar to his own was swooping down, and he could see the vari-coloured circles on her planes which told him she was British. And she was but a few hundred feet above him, yet coming down swiftly as a stone drops.

But would she get down in time to rescue him before that band of yelling Turks reached him? Smylie did not know: all that he did know was that they should never touch his machine. The trouble was that the descending aeroplane might alight so near the stricken machine that when the explosion took place it might be damaged and its pilot be wounded. Lieutenant Smylie, clear-eyed, clear-headed, was watching the one small bomb that remained in place, and, his revolver ready in his hand, he ran back, determined to blow the machine, and any who got near her, into smithereens: never should his British 'plane fall into the enemy's hands.

The hum of the coming aeroplane had now turned to a thunderous roar, and the airman knew that it could be but a few feet from the ground. Then came a hail:

"Quick, man!"

And the aviator shot—shot with an accuracy that was amazing; there was a sharp explosion, a cloud of smoke, a rain of wreckage—and the advancing Turks saw nothing of their anticipated prize but scraps of wood and steel.

But they saw something that made them frenzied; the second aeroplane was on the ground, and the stranded airman was sitting across the fuselage, there being no other place for him to sit. In the brief moments that had elapsed between the firing of the revolver and the descent of the shattered wreckage he had swung his comrade's propeller, had called contact, and had leaped astride the fuselage at the moment the big bird was on the rise.

There was a rush by the Turks, who were yelling excitedly; incredible though it may seem, not one of them fired a shot at the aviators, who could have been killed outright. Instead, they tried to seize the biplane, as though they would pull her down to earth once more. One or two, indeed, did manage to snatch hold of her tail as she quivered to the purring engine, but they were shaken off like so many rats, and up into the clear blueness the biplane went with her double burden—up and out seaward, with the shrapnel bursting all around her. The rescuer—it was Flight-Squadron-Commander Richard Bell-Davies—sat grimly in his seat and manoeuvred his machine into the heights of safety, while the rescued held on grimly to the fuselage with hands and feet.

Commander Davies later received the V.C., and Lieutenant Smylie the D.S.O., and the announcement of the awards referred to the affair as "a feat of airmanship that can seldom have been equalled for skill and gallantry."

Captain S. Grant-Dalton (Yorks and R.F.C.), on escort duty with a raiding party in Egypt, was returning home at the head of his flock, when one of the machines went gliding to earth, badly mauled by gun-fire.

The Turkish gunners had been able to get in a good deal of practice, seeing that the British air-forces had not been idle. So their shooting was not so bad, as Second-Lieutenant Paris, observer to Captain Grant-Dalton, realized when he heard the scream of flying shells, and what was worse, saw the British machine go dropping to earth. Lieutenant Paris promptly informed his pilot of the mishap and the captain instantly made up his mind. The machine must not be allowed to be captured by the Turks. It was evident that its pilot was unable to get it to rise, for through his binoculars Captain Grant-Dalton could see him labouring bravely but vainly trying to get it to start. There was nothing for it, Captain Grant-Dalton decided, but to slide down those intangible precipices, bomb the stranded machine, and carry off its pilot.

Scarcely had Lieutenant Paris realized what was in his pilot's mind, when the machine was diving headlong to earth, the wind whistling as it rushed past, and the Turks playing a rare game with their 'Archies,' striving valiantly and perseveringly to get the range, the speed of the aeroplane making that no easy matter. This was lucky, for it helped the airmen and their machine to run the destructive gauntlet, and they succeeded in landing on the ground near to the derelict 'plane.

It did not take long for Captain Grant-Dalton to put his plans into action. Having satisfied himself that the fallen machine could not be made to fly again in the time at his disposal, he rendered it utterly useless to the Turks, who he knew would soon be hurrying up to take possession of the booty. Then with a cheery smile he took the pilot of the destroyed machine aboard his own and carried him safely away from danger to the home aerodrome.

The venue of the little thrill which we are about to record is given vaguely enough as "the Eastern theatre of war," and the names of the two officers concerned are hidden behind the initials M. and F. However, the absence of names cannot detract from the dramatic interest of the story.

The story runs that Captain M. and Captain F. went up on separate machines to spy out the land and to take photographs of a certain position. Long before they reached their objective, they sighted two black dots which they very quickly identified as enemy machines. This meant that the course of good photography would not run smoothly, because the pilots of those black-cross machines would have to be reckoned with. Not that the British pilots particularly objected to a few extra foes, and, as a matter of fact, to have a 'scrap' in midair is a much better way of passing the time than to be 'strafed' by some foolish gunners in safety beneath you.

So the British sailed in gaily with Lewis guns ready for the fray, although they decided to allow their enemies to go on with their patrol unmolested as long as, in their turn, they themselves were permitted to take photographs. But this did not meet with the approval of their enemies, who made for the two British machines, and a most exciting few minutes followed, during which the aeroplanes made circles around their opponents, or climbed high or drove low—and always the machine-guns *rat-tatted* at one another as they passed. The time came when the foe decided they had had enough for one day, and with a parting drum they turned and made off, much to the delight of the Britons, who thought they could now proceed with their interrupted snapshotting.

But man proposes and a bullet in a petrol tank disposes, as Captain F. discovered. The engine spluttered and tried to work, but finally gave up in despair, and Captain F., positively sick over his hard luck, began to spiral down. Below were many ant-like figures, who were no doubt hugely delighted at the spectacle of their enemy in forced descent, for they thought that presently he would have to land and be compelled to surrender both himself and his machine.

But those men did not know of what stuff Captain F. was made, and they did not know that while he was corkscrewing through the air he was working out a plan to frustrate his foes, vowing that they should never lay hands upon his machine or the photographs he had taken.

Neither did the waiting enemies know that the pilot of the untouched machine had also formed a plan which, if it were successful, would rob them of every scrap of self-satisfaction.

Captain F. came to earth as lightly as a bird, jumped out of his aeroplane, and looked it over quickly to see if it was at all possible to tinker it up and so slip away before the enemy, whom he could see within a short distance rushing toward him, could come up. He found that there was no chance of doing anything in the time at his disposal, and, determined to snatch one prize at least from the foe, he deliberately set fire to the derelict machine. The leaping flames and the rising cloud of smoke told the approaching foe what had happened, and with yells of rage they increased their speed, hoping to arrive in time to put out the fire.

Captain F. stood near his burning mount, waiting for the moment to come when he would have to surrender. But that moment never came. There was a droning roar overhead, and looking up he saw the machine piloted by Captain M. dropping toward him. Instantly he realized what his comrade intended, and needless to say his heart beat quickly as the significance of it burst upon him. The running enemies were so near now that it seemed impossible for Captain M. to reach his friend in time to pick him up, and to fail meant the capture of the heroic Captain F.

The aeroplane came to earth near to Captain F. and its pilot gave a shout of "Hurry!"—as though the- stranded aviator would need any exhortation! He dashed over the intervening yards as though on the running track at school, and in a moment was beside the now stationary 'plane. No time for thanks yet—action, not words, was desired. Because there was no other safe place to which he could scramble in time, Captain F., without undue flurry, mounted the engine cowl and sat on it. Instantly Captain M. let out his engine, and speeding along the ground for some distance his machine mounted into the air. The enemy, shouting and roaring, tore madly toward the escaping prey, and were only 200 yards away when the machine rose like a bird, one man manipulating the 'joy-stick' and levers and the other clinging on to the cowl!

CHAPTER 11

Tales of the Coast Patrol

The navy which had for years toasted 'The Day' when it should hold a reckoning with the sea-dogs of Britain scurried to harbour when the war-clouds burst, confining its activities to an occasional dash upon unfortified towns or harmless fishing vessels, save for a few raiders that managed to elude British watchfulness and the submarines that were to open a new chapter of f rightfulness. When the High Seas Fleet did come out in force at Jutland [1] it was defeated. The Germans, therefore, so far as the North Sea is concerned, have done little more than patrol the Belgian coast behind the shelter of their minefield. But, even these patrol vessels have not been left in unchallenged possession of the small area of water, for the naval airmen of Britain have on several occasions swooped out of the blue depths of sky and fearlessly attacked them.

Such encounters are symbolical of the new methods of warfare and provide the naval counterpart of the spectacular incidents which have taken place every day on land. The fight of a seaplane, piloted by Flight-Sub-Lieutenant James Ferrand, R.N., on November 28th, 1915, against great odds well illustrates the point.

Ferrand, with First-Class Air Mechanic Oldfield as gunner, was on patrol duty off the Belgian coast when he suddenly sighted a German seaplane, for which he made, only to discover that the foe was not alone, but had four other machines keeping it company, while far below on the wintry waters of the North Sea there was an escorting destroyer.

To many men such odds would have been sufficient to justify a hasty retreat, for, after all, there is such a thing as discretion! But to

---

1. *Kiel and Jutland* by Georg von Hase also published by Leonaur.

Ferrand the idea did not occur: he reasoned that if there were so many seaplanes about, with a destroyer escort, it was not at all unlikely that work was afoot the execution of which must be prevented if possible. So, with Oldfield ready with his gun, the lieutenant drove his machine at full speed toward the nearest Hun.

As the two machines came within firing distance the British gunner let rip a whole drum, and then, as the German replied, Ferrand dived, then circled and sped upward again to get position, and Oldfield rammed in a second drum, which he fired as rapidly as his gun would work literally riddling the German seaplane. The enemy machine gave a convulsive shudder as the wind caught the planes, now useless, for the engine was ruined and the pilot had no control over it; then, spinning over and over as it went, it dropped toward the water, into which it plunged, sinking immediately.

Meanwhile, the other four seaplanes and the destroyer were at work with their guns, although apparently the seaplanes were not particularly anxious to get to close quarters. What was happening was that the enemy were trying to lure Ferrand nearer to the coast, and in this they succeeded, for, being intent upon tackling the more formidable foe, the British pilot took little heed of the seaplanes and endeavoured to get at the destroyer, which, as soon as its commander judged the time had come, opened with every gun that could be trained upon the Briton. Ferrand handled his machine with great skill, and, circling round, came well over the destroyer, upon which he dropped some bombs. There seemed every prospect of a really good fight with fair results, when from the shore there came a resounding clap as of thunder, followed by another and yet another.

The Germans' ruse had succeeded in drawing the British machine within range of the shore batteries, and their shells came screaming past the seaplane; and now that the odds were greater in their favour, the German seaplanes also swarmed to the attack.

The British machine-gun was worked heroically, bomb after bomb was launched at the destroyer, and the gallant pilot and his mechanic kept up the worthy fight until it was evident that the odds were such that further success was impossible. Then, and then only, did Lieutenant Ferrand turn his seaplane up into the mist above, away from the enemy's guns. On the whole, he had reason to be pleased with what he had accomplished, although not a little disappointed that the heavy shell fire had prevented him from coming to a conclusion with the destroyer. He had also reason to be pleased with the approval of the authorities, who awarded him a D.S.O.

Both aeroplanes and airships have been found of great value as aids in the work performed by the navy in connexion with the German submarine menace. A submerged submarine is invisible to the lookout of a ship, but the airman overhead can distinguish the steel fish at a depth of about thirty feet—sometimes more, sometimes less, according to the state of the weather—and many of the U-boats which sallied out from bases along the Belgian coast owed their capture or destruction to the 'spotting' work of the aviators of Britain and France. Naturally, the Germans became aware, after a time, that their murdercraft could be distinguished, and they made various experiments in colouring: with what success or non-success we must leave untold.

The manner in which a Frenchman and a Briton, flying together in a French biplane, settled accounts with a U-boat which had, no doubt, been preying upon shipping in the North Sea, is typical of many other encounters. It was on a Sunday in 1915, at about half past eleven, that Flight-Sub-Lieutenant Viney, R.N.A.S., and Lieutenant de Sinçay of the French Flying Service, left their aerodrome and set out on a submarine hunt off Nieuport. They were well supplied with suitable bombs, and, by the time they were five miles west of Nieuport, were flying at a height of some 3000 feet.

Looking down, they saw what seemed too good to be true. Two submarines were lying side by side on the surface. The airmen anticipated that immediately the drone of their engine was heard by the German crews the submarines would submerge. To their astonishment, however, this did not happen, and on closer scrutiny the aviators saw gleaming through the water the bright yellow of a sandbank, and they perceived that there was not sufficient depth for the submarines to dive. It was impossible to hope for a more favourable situation, and, prompt to seize their opportunity, the airmen began a quick spiral descent.

As they dropped signs were not wanting that they had been noticed: men slipped inside the hatches, which were shut down quickly, and although they could not dive the submarines began to try to get away before the biplane could draw close enough to drop bombs with effect. Viney and Sinçay held their missiles, preferring not to risk missing, as they might have done had they released from too great a height. This caution allowed one submarine to escape, for it got up speed and zigzagged on the surface in such a way that, although the biplane was right over it on several occasions, there was little chance of hitting it.

The other, however, seemed to be unmanageable. Perhaps her commander was flustered at the thought of that swooping bird of prey hovering so close above him. True, the submarine moved, but though her commander tried every trick that he knew he could not get her outside of the circles which the descending aeroplane was making. Nearer and nearer the biplane dropped, and while one lieutenant piloted, the other kept his eyes fixed upon the squirming submarine, waiting for the moment when he might begin the attack. This moment came when the pilot brought the machine to within 200 yards of the surface directly over the U-boat. There was a sharp click as the releasing gear let slip one of the destructive balls; almost immediately there followed a sharp crash, and the aviators saw that the first bomb had fallen true, hitting the submarine's bridge and crumpling it up.

All the time the biplane was on the move, of course, and as the bomb hit the mark the machine continued in its circuit. Again it came round over the doomed craft and a second bomb was released. There was a second terrific explosion, the aviators saw a great gaping hole torn in the steel skin and the green water rush in. A moment later nothing was to be seen upon the surface but a widely spreading circle of oil, which indicated where the U-boat had sunk.

It was all very quickly done, necessarily so, for not far off were enemy aeroplanes, whose observers might see the circling biplane and realize what was in progress out at sea. However, there was no interference from enemy aviators, and remaining near the spot just long enough to make sure that their prey had been wounded to the death, Viney and Sinçay reascended at full speed to the dizzy altitudes whence they had swooped, and sailed homeward in high spirits, no doubt, at their success.

Following the British official announcement of the thrilling episode, came a wireless from Berlin to the effect that:

> Competent German authorities repeat that no German submarine has been destroyed by a British aeroplane. Papers point out that if the English report is correct, either a British or a French submarine has been destroyed.

No doubt this was reported immediately to the horse-marines!

On May 21st, 1916, a number of German raiding machines suddenly swooped out of the sky and rained their exploding missiles over Dunkirk. News quickly reached a certain aerodrome, and several British machines of the Coast Patrol darted up with the intention of

A SEAPLANE 'SPOTTING' A SUBMARINE

cutting off the raiders as they passed Nieuport on their return.

Flight-Sub-Lieutenant 'Anonymous' of the R.N.A.S., mounted on a Nieuport scout, saw them as black specks in the distance, and went out to meet them, rising till he was in a position to attack and opening fire on them at a range of 400 yards. He sprayed the passing machines and would have continued the fight but for the fact that at that moment he heard the roar of another engine above, and, looking up, saw a black-crossed 'plane at about 300 yards distance and with the advantage of position.

Lieutenant 'Anonymous' at once set his elevators to 'rise' and went after the new enemy, chasing him out to sea until he was within effective range, when he emptied a drum into him. Reloading as quickly as possible and still climbing, the intrepid airman reached a height of 10,000 feet, his eyes still upon the fleeing foe, when he was suddenly attacked by a large two-seater German machine which opened fire at a long range.

One more foe did not matter much to Lieutenant 'Anonymous,' who promptly replied with his Lewis gun. He was able to see that his aim had been remarkably good, even at the long range at which the duel was being fought.

Suddenly smoke began to issue from the German machine, a smother of black cloud which almost hid it from the eyes of the victor, who, not without pleasure, saw the burning 'plane take a nosedive to the sea.

Lieutenant 'Anonymous,' however, had little time to enjoy the results of his triumph and attack, for yet another enemy now appeared. He proceeded to expend the remainder of his ammunition upon the new foe, and the 'scrap' only terminated when he had no more cartridges to fire. The airman now decided that it was high time to be going, and he arrived safely at the aerodrome to learn, that a fellow-pilot had witnessed his fight with the two-seater, a burning example of the prowess and courage of British airmen in general and of Lieutenant 'Anonymous' in particular.

Another anonymous hero of the Coast Patrol had a thrilling tale to tell, when, after the 'scrap' in which he was wounded, he lay on a hospital bed, in blessed contentment at having plentifully 'strafed' several Huns before being put out of action.

The pilot, whose name doubtless has appeared above a three-line paragraph which omitted everything that would serve to make the story real, was out on a bombing expedition over Marcoing (south-west of Cambrai) on August 2nd, 1916, and after having deposited with good effect the steel-cased explosives—the anti-aircraft guns meantime making thunderous music all about him—he banked, turned, and headed for home.

But he was not to be allowed to get away unmolested. The Germans, finding that their batteries were not making good practice, sent up aeroplanes. The first that the unnamed pilot knew of this, however, was when he turned and almost crashed into an L.V.G. scout—one of the latest of its type—which was pelting toward him. It was a close shave, the touch of a lever deciding the fate of both aviators, but the Britisher was equal to the occasion and swept upward, so missing the Hun machine, which went roaring on beneath him. As he passed, the British bomber, his gun already unshipped, emptied a drum into his enemy and quickly slipped in another drum, intending to follow up his attack. While thus attending to his gun, he saw another British pilot bear down upon the German, which probably hurt his feelings, because the warriors of the air have a particular liking for finishing off their foes without assistance.

However, the British officer need not have felt annoyed at the thought of missing a 'scrap,' for, a moment later, a German Roland thundered into action and let fly a stream of missiles at him, to receive a full drum in return as the British machine drove in. That pilot experienced all the excitement he needed—and maybe, although one can never tell with these kings of the air! a little more than that, for while engaged with Hun Roland, a violent storm seemed to crash down upon him. Throwing a quick glance behind him, the pilot saw no fewer than three other Rolands hanging on to his tail and rattling out hundreds of machine-gun bullets.

No matter how the pilot tried to shake them off, they remained poised, as it were, directly over the tail of his machine; and the storm of bullets was unpleasantly steady—far too steady, for one riddled its way into the poor fellow's leg and he had much ado to refrain from yelling with the pain of it. Knowing that more than ever his life depended on keeping cool, he finished slipping in another drum, of which he gave the Rolands the benefit, much to their discomfiture, for the Lewis gun swinging from side to side sprayed them with good British bullets and convinced their pilots that safety lay in putting as great a distance as possible between themselves and their snappy foe.

If they had only known!

Scarcely had the Germans winged out of range than the engine of the stricken pilot began to misfire and thus bang out its protest at being expected to work without a sufficient supply of petrol. The airman, knowing the signs, gave a hasty glance at his tank, and saw a neat little hole, like a black spot, through which the petrol was squirting.

A moment or so later the engine struck, and the pilot, although he knew that to land now would be to fall into the hands of the enemy, had no other course open to him but to make for earth. Sliding down gracefully, but in a frightful temper at the fate that had played him so scurvy a trick, he looked about for a likely landing-place.

The petrol from the tank was flowing over his left leg, and as it soaked through, the pilot had a brilliant idea—he shoved his knee against the hole and so stopped the flow; then, thinking that if he got more pressure he might even yet be able to get the engine to start again, he pumped for all he was worth, glancing anxiously at any movement of the needle of the pressure gauge. Meanwhile the aeroplane had been heading for the ground, which was now only about 200 feet below, with many Germans firing up in the hope of hastening its descent. Suddenly, to the pilot's unfeigned joy, he heard his engine grunt and then open out into a protesting roar. It took but a brief while to flatten out and set the head of the machine for home—about fifteen miles distance, by the way.

It was a thrilling affair. Pumping hard, and keeping his knee over the hole to prevent the petrol from leaking, the pilot kept up the necessary pressure in the tank. It was no easy matter to do the two things and at the same time guide the machine. It was impossible to get the aeroplane to rise, and the intrepid pilot had to content himself with flying at the altitude to which the engine would lift him, about fifty feet.

Several times the engine seemed about to give in again, but pumping harder than ever, the pilot succeeded in keeping on the go. On one of these occasions he gave up hope and had flattened out to land, when suddenly the engine resumed working when only a few feet from the ground, and he was able to shove his machine up a little higher.

By this time the pilot was feeling sick and faint from loss of blood and exhausted through the severe exertion of pumping. As he crossed the German lines machine-guns below opened out upon him and, seeing the low altitude at which he was flying, it was a miracle that he was not hit.

But, in due course, he succeeded in getting away, only to come to a place which he did not know. He was lost, and being so near the ground could not pick out landmarks by which to steer.

At length, however, he saw a French bi-plane flying low. Following it, he saw where it landed and made for the same spot, but went to earth with a crash which damaged his machine badly but fortunately did not injure him. The landing was made just in time; the pilot was almost at the point of collapse and a few more moments might have resulted in disaster.

Before the war, spectators at Flying Exhibitions held their breath as they saw some intrepid airman deliberately make his machine loop the loop. It seemed the acme of foolhardiness, a courting of death, but such experiments—for they were little more—added to our knowledge of the factors which make for air-worthiness, and in the Great War many an aviator has no doubt owed his life to the fact that those who looped the loop lived to tell of certain things which ought to be done to make certain machines more stable. Tucked in among the annals of our Flying Corps are the brief details of a story which, when the whole of it can be told, will be found to excel, in no mere dramatic sense, most things that have happened in the air.

The British pilot—name unknown, unfortunately—mounted in a single-seater scout, was on May 14th, 1915, chasing a German machine, the pilot of which apparently did not like the idea of joining issue with the foe who persisted in hanging on his tail. The German must have been brought to bay but for a queer accident. The British aviator, having splashed out a drum of cartridges, was in the act of reloading his gun when by some misfortune his machine temporarily got out of control. It was only a momentary lapse, but in the air even a second counts, and the aeroplane, without any controlling hand on it, suddenly made a dive and turned completely over, remaining in that position as it tumbled earthward.

A tremendous event that, for the earth was 8000 feet below; and it is not difficult to imagine what thoughts must have flashed through the officer's mind.

That he was not hurled out of the machine to fall, a mangled mass, on the ground, is little less than a miracle, particularly as the safety-belt, with which every airman straps himself into his machine, happened to be loose and had slipped down over his legs. As the aeroplane turned its dramatic somersault, the airman but for his remarkable presence of mind would have gone flying into space.

As the machine turned over the airman clutched the rear centre-section struts and gripped for dear life. The safety-belt held his legs tight as in shackles, and while the machine went on its terrible journey through space, the unfortunate pilot, hanging head downward, clung to the struts and tried to disentangle his legs. Round and round like a *teetotum* the aeroplane spun, and the motion of it sickened the aviator, whose blood ran into his head until he thought it would burst. The strain on his arms was tremendous and his struggles made the machine shiver from wing to wing. He expected any moment to see the wings fold up, and in that case the end would come only too soon. The suspense was awful; no less so because it did not last many seconds. The aviator's life depended upon his getting his legs free of the leather shackles, since the only hope of righting the machine—amazing thing that in such circumstances any man dared even hope to perform such a miracle!—lay in reaching the control levers with his feet. With eyes staring, and above him only the blurred mass of his overturned mount, with his heart almost stopping, and yet, as well as man can be in such a position, clear headed and of set purpose, the airman exerted all his efforts, used all his cunning, and at last, with a gasp of relief, felt first one leg and then the other slip out of the strap.

He did not know how near the ground he might be; all he knew was that he must have fallen a tremendous distance, and that his chance of life lay in immediate action. His legs sought and found the control lever up there in the fuselage, the control wires worked, ailerons moved, the elevators of the machine answered to the call, and, miracle of miracles! the aeroplane began to bend over, as it were, stood almost on its nose, then tilted, and at last rose up and fell back into position.

And the airman found himself in his seat, into which, as the machine righted itself, he had automatically dropped, though he still clutched the thin spar of salvation.

When in due time he returned to earth the much-tried pilot had survived an experience the like of which few men have passed through and come back to tell the tale.

One of the most dramatic episodes of the Coast Patrol occurred on July 15th, 1916. One of our Naval flying men, who had left Dunkirk, was ten miles off the coast and some 12,000 feet high when, as he was approaching Ostend, he encountered a German seaplane, which was flying about 500 feet below him.

The recognition was simultaneous, and there began a matching of wits for position. The German seaplane, a single-engined tractor, banked and turned suddenly with intent to get into position behind

The R.N.A.S. at work a seaplane duel off the Belgian coast

and below the Naval machine. A second later both machines were executing a steep glide, and but for the promptitude of the Briton the German would have succeeded in obtaining the tactical advantage. There was but one way to counter the German's move, and the Briton, with swift decision, determined to loop the loop over his opponent. Down went his ailerons at the bidding of the control wires, and the aeroplane, to the amazement, no doubt, of the German (who probably imagined that his enemy had lost control), dipped, then rose again, and swept up and round, until it turned completely over. When the British machine righted itself, the seaplane had passed underneath it, and from his favourable position behind the British pilot opened fire at a range of 100 yards.

It was quickly evident that some of the bullets had got home, for the German pilot, apparently wounded, lost control, and his seaplane tipped over into a vertical nosedive. The petrol tank must have been holed, for as the seaplane fell it caught fire, and the British pilot's last vision of it was of a flaming torch heading for the depths of the North Sea.

CHAPTER 12

A Batch of V.C.s

Like the other branches of the fighting forces, the Royal Flying Corps and the Royal Naval Air Service have won their quota of Victoria Crosses in the war, and in other chapters will be found the stories of the marvellous feats by which some of them were won. It goes without saying that the V.C. is not won easily, as the following accounts of almost superhuman bravery will show.

Major Lance G. Hawker (R.E. and R.F.C.), who won his Victoria Cross on July 25th, 1915, had about three months previously been awarded the D.S.O. for a dash over the German lines to Gontrode, where he attacked an airship shed. The 'Archies' were very active that particular day, and a ring of bursting shells seemed to be made around the devoted airman as he droned within sight of the Germans. He had been unable to take them by surprise, for over the position was a captive balloon, the occupants of which had heard and seen the oncoming aeroplane long before the men at the guns had done so, and had telephoned the news to those below. But Lieutenant Hawker (he was lieutenant in those days) had not gone out on his expedition without knowing that he had a difficult task before him, and the balloon which had enabled the Germans to prepare a warm welcome for him was destined to assist him in his work, for as he sailed into view of it the intrepid airman by a stroke of genius decided to use the 'sausage' as a shield.

He was flying at a great height as he approached the shed, but knowing that in order to drop his bombs effectively he must get closer to his objective, the airman presently began to descend at a speed which completely baffled the gunners. As he drew nearer he very skilfully manoeuvred so that he had the balloon between his machine and the artillery. This, of course, added to the difficulties of the German gunners, who, naturally, had no wish to send a screaming shell into the giant gas-bag, from which was suspended a basket containing some of their own comrades. The lieutenant found that dodging the shells was no easy task, even when he was at a great height, and when in due course he came within 200 feet of the ground, it is not too much to say that it was a case of 'touch and go.'

Indeed, it was remarkable that his machine was not smashed to pieces. Only the utmost ingenuity in the utilization of that captive balloon saved the airman from destruction and enabled him to wing into such a position that he could loose his bombs with such a degree of accuracy that they went crashing on to the airship shed, to the consternation of the Germans who had felt sure of their prey. The lieutenant was within so short a distance of the shed that he felt the effects of his own bombs; but, cool-headed and calm, he kept his machine under complete control and, while the 'Archies' boomed out at him, he set his aeroplane climbing back into the giddy heights and so away toward home. In such fashion did he win the D.S.O. And now to relate the manner in which he earned the little bronze Maltese cross—"For Valour."

The official announcement of the award began with, "For most conspicuous bravery and very great ability," and, as the powers that be do not indulge in superlatives without ample reason, it is evident that the exploit of Major Hawker, although officially described in a ten-line notice, was something fairly remarkable, to say the least. What really happened, so far as we are permitted to know, was that on July 25th, Major Hawker was flying on reconnaissance duty "somewhere in France," when suddenly he was attacked simultaneously by three enemy aeroplanes. The odds were greater than would at first appear, for each of the hostile battle-planes carried a pilot and an observer, both of whom had machine-guns, while the gallant major was flying alone. It really meant, therefore, six men to one and six guns to one, and yet Major Hawker went gaily into the 'scrap.'

At a height of 10,000 feet he bore down upon one of the machines, leaving the others to do as they liked while he attended to their companion. Needless to say, the two companion machines tried their best to bring him down, but Major Hawker concentrated his efforts upon the one he had marked, and, after a short yet severe tussle, he peppered the German 'plane all over, so badly mauling it that its pilot lost control and had to make a dive for the ground, where, unfortunately for him, he landed with a crash inside the British lines.

While his crippled opponent was slipping through airy spaces. Major Hawker was at grips with a second one, and, despite a tremendous *ta-ta-ta-tatting* of the two machine-guns mounted on it, and the whistling of bullets from the third machine which he could not tackle for a little while, he manoeuvred his aeroplane with such marked ability that from the beginning it was evident the Huns were outmatched. Before very long the major saw the second hostile machine bank, turn, and then swoop away, heading for its own lines. It had been so severely handled that its pilot had all his work cut out to keep control, but succeeded in doing so just long enough to reach safety.

It was now time to deal with number three, which Major Hawker treated as he had the other two. He tackled it with vigour, poured in a rapid fire of shots which tore through the wings and the body, generally making things so warm for the two German airmen that, not at all relishing their treatment and by no means eager to suffer the fate of their companions, they turned and scurried away, hotly pursued by Major Hawker, who, however, was unable to bring them again to action.

Since the days when the major performed that feat many other airmen have done similar things, and very many have been faced by even greater odds; yet it must be remembered that in the early part of 1915 aerial fighting may be said to have been in its infancy: machines were not so air-worthy, the armament of them was not so effective, and altogether the danger and the difficulty were relatively greater. With the improvements made in aircraft, such an affair as a fight between one machine and three became more or less a minor matter, but that in nowise diminishes the achievement of Major Hawker, who at later dates distinguished himself yet more, and won the reputation of being one of Britain's finest aerial fighters. Without much doubt, the reports of the Air Board made reference to his name in their repeated commendations of 'Major A.' and 'Major B.' To the regret of very many, in 1916 his name appeared in the list of 'Missing.'

About a week after Major Hawker had won the V.C, one of his fellow-fliers. Captain John Aidan Liddell (3rd Argyll and Sutherland Highlanders and R.F.C.), also won the distinction. On the last day of July, 1915, Captain Liddell was on a flying reconnaissance over Ostend-Bruges-Ghent, when he was wounded in the thigh by high-explosive shrapnel from an anti-aircraft gun. His leg was riddled with bullets, being wounded in fifty places! The observer, who saw his pilot sag helplessly, and realized that he was sorely wounded, had little time for thinking, for the aeroplane immediately began to drop sheer down. The shock had rendered Captain Liddell unconscious, and he had been jammed between the steering-wheel and the side of his seat. The machine was free to go its own way—which was directly earthward—and the jerk pitched the observer between the struts and the machine-gun. As the aeroplane dropped the rush of the wind was tremendous, and the observer was never so thankful in his life for being jammed up so that he could not move, for the machine turned turtle and then came right way up again, as it dropped in a spin from which it appeared there could be no recovery!

The unconscious pilot, it seemed, would never come back to the world of feeling. The observer well knew what happened in such circumstances: he had seen machines crash to earth when the pilot had lost control. There is on record the story of two airmen who found themselves in a similar plight to that in which Captain Liddell and his comrade were in, and the observer, unable to do anything to right the machine, had to content himself with trying to rouse his pilot by banging as loudly as he could upon the framework of the aeroplane! Whether that had any effect, or whether it was the uprush of cold air which brought the pilot back to consciousness, is not known, but the fact remains that after the uncontrolled machine had dropped 5000 feet, and when it was within 2000 feet of the ground, the pilot regained consciousness, and succeeded in getting his mount under control again.

In like manner. Captain Liddell came round, to find himself bleeding profusely, with a feeling that if he moved his leg would drop off; with pain racking his body, his head throbbing, and his machine slipping downward at a speed amazing even to so skilled an airman. The altimeter showed they had fallen 3000 feet, and it seemed impossible for him to pull up, because in the moment that his eyes opened he saw that the control wheel was affected. How could he hope to get his machine in hand? He could see no way to do so, and yet—such is the stuff of which heroes are made—he attempted the seemingly impossible.

Only Captain Liddell himself knows how he managed it, but the fact remains that, growing weaker and weaker every second, and scarcely able to bear the pain, by fumbling about in a half-dazed way with levers which did not want to move, he succeeded at last in getting the engine to answer. The elevators worked and, with a convulsive shiver, as though resenting the insolence of man daring to control it, the aeroplane began to slacken its pace, pushed up its nose, and approached something like an even keel.

Down below, German gunners who had seen the headlong drop of the machine and expected to see it crash itself to pieces on the ground, were amazed to see it begin to fly normally again. The whole thing seemed incredible. Yet, that did not prevent them, naturally, from doing their very best to bring it down after all; for, as Captain Liddell turned toward the Belgian lines, where, many miles away, was an aerodrome, the anti-aircraft guns opened fire, and the cotton-wool whorls appeared on every side. The gallant captain—who knew that he could not last long, because of the stream of blood which was dyeing his machine red—fought against the desire to lapse once more into a blissful state of unconsciousness, fought, not merely for his own sake, but for the sake of the man who looked to him to drive the machine back to safety, and for the sake of the authorities who waited somewhere behind the line for the report which had been gathered during the first part of the tragic flight.

Fortunately, he did not fight in vain. The official announcement ran:

> Notwithstanding his collapsed state, he succeeded, although continually fired at, in completing his course, and brought the aeroplane into our lines, half an hour after he had been wounded. . . .
> The difficulties experienced by this officer in saving his machine, and the life of his observer, cannot readily be expressed, but as the control wheel and throttle control were smashed, and also one of the undercarriage struts, it would seem incredible that he could have accomplished his task.

Praise indeed: and heroism indeed!

"You must lift me out," Captain Liddell said to those who rushed to his assistance as he brought the machine to earth. "If I move, I am afraid my leg will drop off."

He was carried to hospital, but, although everything possible was done for him, he did not live to receive the Victoria Cross, which was placed on his bier.

The official announcement of the award of the Victoria Cross to Second-Lieutenant Gilbert S. M. Insall (R.F.C.) stated that it was bestowed "For most conspicuous bravery, skill, and determination," and the high praise was well deserved.

This gallant officer was on patrol duty on November 7th, 1915, and his watch in the air was after a while rewarded by the appearance of a German aeroplane. The meeting between the aviators took place near Achiet, toward which town the British airman chased the German, who apparently disliked the look of the big Vickers fighting machine in which Insall was mounted. With his engine putting forth every possible ounce of power, the Teuton sped through the air; but he could not shake off the Vickers 'plane, which hung relentlessly at his tail. Finding that he could not escape, the German aviator changed his course and, although Insall did not know it until it was too late, lured him toward a hidden battery.

The stern chase continued, and at last the two aeroplanes were almost over the battery. The first inkling Insall had of the danger was a salvo from the guns below; but, with remarkable coolness, he dived from a giddy height until he was almost touching the German machine. His gunner, First-Class Air Mechanic T. H. Donald, was on the *qui vive*, waiting eagerly for the moment when he could effectively let loose a stream of bullets at the fleeing foe; that moment came, and Donald, taking cool aim as his machine swooped down, opened fire. A whole drum of cartridges was scattered upon the rival machine, and the marksmanship was so good that its engine was hit and stopped dead.

The German was now in a sorry plight, but he knew that he had still a chance of escape if he could but volplane to earth before his antagonist regained position and attacked him again. Below was a thick bank of cloud, and into this, and through it, the German dropped. Caring nothing for the danger that he knew must lie on the other side of the cloud, Insall also dived into the mist-veil, and, emerging from it, saw his enemy still going earthward. Like a hawk pouncing upon its prey the British machine swooped down, a few breathless seconds ensued, and then Donald once more opened fire, spraying the German machine with a nickel hail which literally shattered it, sending it hurtling into a ploughed field a few miles south-east of Arras. By little short of a miracle the aviators escaped death. When their machine landed, they scrambled out and very pluckily prepared to engage the Vickers 'plane, now hovering close above them.

Insall, when he saw that the Germans were still bent on fighting, dropped yet lower, till within 500 feet above the spot where the wrecked machine lay. From this position Donald let his machine-gun rip out its tattoo of death, and the Germans finding the place too hot for them wisely took to their heels. One of them was wounded, but his comrade gallantly kept with him and tried to help him along to safety.

The British airmen, having defeated their foes, now turned their attention to the destruction of the machine itself. Near at hand were German trenches, the occupants of which were firing rapidly at the Vickers machine, which, however, merely completed its circle, and, as it again passed over the German machine, loosed an incendiary bomb from its rack. There was a sharp report, a burst of flame and smoke, and as he swept round and up Insall's last glance showed the enemy machine a total wreck.

The problem now before the victors was how to get home. They were about 2000 feet above the ground, and in order to obtain a higher speed than they were flying at, it was necessary to dive down. This, however, meant that they would come within easier range of German riflemen in the trenches over which they must pass; but the plucky Britishers took the risk, and improved the occasion. To the utter astonishment of the Germans, the aeroplane swooped toward them, the roar of the engine sounding like thunder. They could not understand such tactics, and they could not imagine what the airmen intended. They were soon enlightened, however, for as the British machine came over the trenches its machine-gun opened fire, and Donald raked the defence ditches with disastrous effects upon their occupants.

Even as the aeroplane passed Insall pulled up and set his elevators to rise, and as the machine responded it was followed by a terrific burst of fire from the Germans, who had speedily recovered from their surprise. Bullets whistled past the rising aeroplane, cut holes in its planes and nacelle, and—worst luck of all—penetrated the petrol tank. Insall, looking at his gauge, realized that the oil was running out. To an aeroplane, oil is what the blood is to the body, and the Lieutenant knew that he must extract from his engine all he possibly could within the next few minutes if he were to get his machine to safety. He resolved not to try to fly to his station, but to alight just within the British lines.

Scanning the country beneath and before him, he saw a wood not far away, which he judged to be about 500 yards within the British lines, and thereabout he decided to land. From behind him, as he drove onward, German anti-aircraft guns continued to fire, and bursting shrapnel created smoke-clouds in all directions, but the speed at which the Vickers machine was flying and the fact that it was now gliding earthward disconcerted the gunners, so that nothing happened to prevent Insall from guiding his machine gracefully to rest beyond the friendly wood.

The moment the aeroplane touched earth Insall and his mechanic jumped out to see what they could do with the petrol tank. If they had hoped to be left unmolested, they were disappointed; for the Germans, who had realized the purpose of the airmen, promptly opened fire in the direction in which the aeroplane had dropped. During the next few hours no fewer than a hundred and fifty shells were dropped, fired at the machine, but not one of them caused any material damage. In the face of the bombardment, however, Insall and his companion found it impossible to effect repairs during daylight, and so they waited in the wood until night fell. Then, by the aid of screened lights, they overhauled their machine, and found it badly knocked about by rifle fire but still in a repairable condition. It took them nearly all night to effect these repairs, but at last they were done, and at the break of day Insall and Donald mounted their aerial steed again, taxied it along the ground, and then drummed their way upward and homeward, duly reaching their station little the worse for their perilous adventure.

In another place we have told the story of a dive to earth in a machine that was a mass of flames, and here in this collection of tales about the V.C. we must include that of Sergeant Thomas Mottershead of the R.F.C., who passed through the terrifying experience of dropping to earth in a blazing aeroplane.

It was one day in 1917 that Sergeant Mottershead pushed up the nose of his machine and drove to a height of 9000 feet, to enable Lieutenant Gower, his companion, to make observations of certain points in the enemy lines. Hostile machines came out to meet the target-marked 'plane, and a very severe little 'scrap' took place nearly two miles above the ground. The Britishers were unfortunate, for a machine-gun in one of the enemy 'planes sprayed the aeroplane with bullets and tore a hole in the petrol tank.

Instantly, the fuel began to flow out and down toward the engine. Lieutenant Gower saw the first flash as the liquid caught light, and he immediately endeavoured to beat out the fire. It is no easy matter, however, to subdue flaming petrol, and Gower realized that the position was very serious.

Sergeant Mottershead realized this also, and knew that it was useless to think of continuing the fight. If he were to save the life of his observer, whose information was wanted by those in command below, he must immediately make for earth, trusting to the powers who guard airmen that Lieutenant Gower might be able to triumph over the fire. There seemed little likelihood of that, however, seeing that the descent would have to be made at top speed, which would cause the air to fan the flames until they enveloped the whole aeroplane.

This was just what happened as the intrepid pilot sent his aerial mount plunging for earth. The flowing petrol ran into the flames already kindled, the air, as the machine rushed through it, drove the flames up to the tank, and before many minutes had passed the aeroplane was a blazing torch, with a stream of fire leaping behind it and a trail of black smoke.

A fearful sight to watch, and a fearful experience for the aviators! Throughout the time the machine was falling, Lieutenant Gower gallantly fought the flames, which he noticed were being fanned by the air all around the legs of the gallant pilot; but his efforts were unavailing.

Grim-faced, cool-headed, Mottershead sat in his seat, with the flames scorching his uniform and burning his legs horribly—the legs that he could not move out of the way because they were controlling the machine; and through the flames he was looking for a safe landing-place.

He was suffering intensely; the pain must have been sufficient to drive an ordinary man mad, and the whole incident was terrific in its horror. Yet the gallant sergeant did not lose his head: one thought only was present, and that was that he must save Lieutenant Gower.

The machine was slithering down the airy spaces at a wonderful speed, thousands of feet were dropped in an incredibly short time, and Sergeant Mottershead now realized that he must begin to flatten out for the landing, in order to avoid a dive into the ground. That this man could control himself to think clearly in such circumstances is astounding, and speaks volumes for his courage.

When Mottershead saw what he judged was a likely place for landing, he flattened as well as he could, considering the speed at which the machine was travelling and the fact that some of its control wires had been burnt away like so many cotton strands. It was a moment filled with tense anxiety and dread possibilities. Sergeant Mottershead, despite his bravery, was almost at the breaking-point: his eyes were bleared, the pain in his legs was terrible. Just behind him the tank was blazing, making life unendurable. It seemed easier and better to die than to live.

Then the climax that he had dreaded happened. During that wild, mad descent the thought had ever been present that, as the struts had been burnt away, the machine might at any moment collapse; perhaps the tail might drop off, and then . . . the result was too awful to contemplate. Fortunate it was for that gallant pilot and his observer that the catastrophe happened when the machine was within only a short distance of the ground; otherwise, neither would have escaped death by being crashed to earth. Even as it was, when the aeroplane suddenly collapsed to the ground, a flaming mass still, Sergeant Mottershead was pinned down by the wreckage, and only by the promptitude of some soldiers who had watched the awesome spectacle was he brought out alive and conveyed to hospital, to die, alas! before the world learned of his brilliant exploit.

> Though suffering extreme torture from burns Sergeant Mottershead showed the most conspicuous presence of mind in the careful selection of a landing-place, and his wonderful endurance and fortitude undoubtedly saved the life of his observer.

Thus testified the official announcement chronicling the posthumous award of the V.C. to this gallant pilot.

Chapter 13

The Man who Brought Down Immelmann

The aerial war has produced some fine fighters amongst the various belligerents, though it fell to the lot of the German aviators to be given personal credit long before the British airmen were allowed to be known as gallant and successful fighters in the air. Day after day the Berlin *communiqués* reported that Lieutenant So-and-So had brought down his *n*th. enemy machine; but although many British pilots had quite as fine totals notched to their credit, they were hidden behind the anonymity of Lieutenant A, or Squadron-Commander B. Amongst the German air heroes was Lieutenant Immelmann, whose prowess the Teutons were forever singing; they were never weary of proclaiming to the world each victory gained by him. There came a day, however, when Immelmann fought his last fight—fought it as became the brave man that he was.

Yet, amazing to relate, the man who vanquished this valiant fighter figured in dispatches for some time simply as "Lieutenant M'C." Naturally, questions were asked when the news of what was one of the greatest air fights of the war filtered through, and a demand was made that the identity of the hero should be disclosed. Tardily, the information was given, and the world which was thrilled by the story, even when robbed of its personal features, re-read it with deepened interest when it was revealed that the conqueror was Second-Lieutenant M'Cubbin, R.F.C.

Before telling the story of Lieutenant Immelmann's tragic end, however, it might be as well to recite the tale of a typical encounter with him. It is based upon a letter written by one of the British aviators who took part in it, Lieutenant Slade, who was taken prisoner at the end of the combat.

This fine young officer was acting as observer to Captain Darley of the R.F.C, and the pair were flying, in a French-built machine, over the German lines when, suddenly, and as it were from nowhere, a Fokker appeared.

Immelmann, the champion Fokker pilot of Germany, was mounted in that sinister-looking monoplane, and, following his customary tactics, he came up from behind the Britishers and they had no knowledge of his presence until he was pouring in a stream of bullets, which lierally riddled the petrol tank, and made it about as useful as a sieve for holding petrol. Captain Darley, the instant he realized what was taking place, endeavoured to get out of range of the deadly stream by tipping his machine on to its nose, in the hope that the bullets would go slithering past, and thus allow him to manoeuvre for position from which to fight the hovering foe.

Immelmann, however, was master of his machine, and had perfected his system of attack. The *rat-tat-tat* of his machine-gun went on, and many of the bullets found their mark. Captain Darley felt a stinging pain in his right arm, and knew that a bullet had passed through it; the thumb of his left hand stopped a shot which absolutely smashed it. But by a perfect miracle Lieutenant Slade, although his clothes were riddled with bullets, escaped injury. When he saw the plight of his pilot, he pulled out his penknife, leaned over, and performed a surgical operation in midair, amputating Captain Darley's thumb, the while that Immelmann was keeping in deadly line with the descending British aeroplane and giving it the full benefit of belt after belt, until he was assured that there was no chance of the Britishers escaping. Then, like the chivalrous foe that he was—and there was not a man of the British Flying Services but had a fine appreciation of the sporting instincts of Immelmann—he desisted from firing, contenting himself with flying within range and watching his enemies make their descent.

Flight was out of the question, for the petrol was leaking badly from the tank, and the great danger was that which every man of the air most dreads; it was quite on the cards that the escaping fuel might set fire to the machine, and the occupants be cremated as it fell a blazing mass. Fortunately for the captain and his companion this terrible thing did not happen, and although Captain Darley had been wounded again in the left hand, so that it was quite useless, he was able with his right arm to keep control of the machine, guiding it toward the earth, where he made an admirable landing.

The instant the machine came to earth Lieutenant Slade leapt out with the idea of setting fire to the aeroplane before German soldiers could rush up and capture it. Immelmann, however, had landed almost simultaneously and, knowing that the aviators would endeavour to destroy their machine, he hurried over, and claimed the pair as prisoners and their machine as just trophy. There was, of course, nothing to be done but to surrender in the circumstances, and, after all, the unpleasant task was rendered less galling by the courtesy of the German, who did all he possibly could for the Britishers. Lieutenant Slade, writing and describing the experience, made reference to his enemy in these terms: "He is a gentleman, and if ever we capture him I hope he will be treated as such."

It was not to be Immelmann's fortune to be taken prisoner; he was destined to die while engaged in the work of which he had become a past master.

His last great battle took place in July 1 916, and it is interesting to note that his antagonist, Second-Lieutenant M'Cubbin, had never been in an aeroplane before the February of that year.

Lieutenant M'Cubbin went up in an F.E. machine between eight and nine o'clock, and was accompanied by three other battle-planes, one of them piloted by Lieutenant Savage. The duty in hand was what the official report termed "an offensive patrol"—that is, a trip to bomb anything within the enemy lines worth bombing, and at the same time deal with any hostile aeroplanes met with.

When several thousand feet up, the British airmen sighted a squadron of no fewer than eleven enemy 'planes, including L.V.G.s, Rolands, and Fokkers. Long odds, those! But M'Cubbin and his comrades welcomed the opportunity for a good fight, and sailed into it with one heart. The leading Britisher made a dive for an L.V.G., which promptly turned tail and headed away east. Thus foiled, the British airman swooped down at a Fokker, there was a brisk interchange of shots, much manoeuvring—and down to earth went the Fokker. Thereupon one of the Rolands attacked; another short, sharp encounter followed—and the Roland went to keep its companion company on the ground.

Meanwhile, the second British machine had joined issue with a Roland. There was the usual manoeuvring for position, much rat- tatting of machine-guns, and this Roland also, put out of control, went hurtling to earth. In the midst of this particular fight, two Fokkers, seeing that their comrade was in a tight corner and likely to be beaten, came humming through the air, intent on smashing the Britishers. So anxious were they, however, that they narrowly missed destruction themselves, only the skill and coolness of their pilots averting a collision in midair. This little episode in the drama resulted in their being too late to assist the doomed Roland.

M'Cubbin flying at 8000 feet had witnessed these various incidents, and was hurrying to the attack, when he caught sight of three Fokkers hovering some 5000 feet above him, and about to swoop down to attack Lieutenant Savage. The latter was ready for them, and when the first Fokker appeared he assailed it vigorously and skilfully, sending it down in a spinning nosedive. Scarcely had he disposed of this foe when he was attacked by the other two Fokkers, which came sweeping down toward him. Fokkers being designed for sudden descents and fitted with fixed machine-guns which spray their bullets as the machine swoops down, it was necessary for Lieutenant Savage to, out-manoeuvre his opponents; so, to avoid that first rush, and to be ready to attack the Fokkers when opportunity offered, he suddenly dived to within 5500 feet of the ground. M'Cubbin realized what was in Savage's mind, and determined to go to his assistance, although this called for a sheer drop of 2500 feet if he was to get into the zone of the battle.

Down went the Fokkers, straight and steady as stones dropped from a balloon, and following them in the wild dramatic dive was M'Cubbin. The machine-guns on the Fokkers were spitting viciously, and M'Cubbin saw Savage's machine suddenly swerve dangerously. He knew what had happened; the leading Fokker, diving headlong for the tail of the British battle-plane, had pelted it with nickel missiles, one of which had evidently caught the gallant Savage. The British pilot lost control of his machine, the engine of which had also been hit, and he plunged down to earth and died the death of a defeated airman. The Fokker which had brought about this disaster was piloted by the redoubtable Immelmann, who had once more played his dangerous trick of spraying shots as he swooped; but he was to play the trick no more.

M'Cubbin, dropping plumb for his foe, reached him before he had time to right the Fokker after the triumphant encounter. Another man might have given the order to fire while still at a safe distance, but M'Cubbin, knowing that he could rely upon the nerves of his observer, who was manning the machine-gun, and knowing too that as the Fokker's gun was fixed it could not be brought to bear unless the machine turned, sailed close into Immelmann while the latter was still trying to complete the wide circle which should bring him into position to attack.

The great moment came when the F.E. and Fokker were close together, so close that they were almost touching each other, and then M'Cubbin's observer fired. That encounter took place at something less than a thousand feet above ground, and the first round ended the battle. M'Cubbin's machine was driving, like a wheel within a wheel, alongside the unfortunate Immelmann, who, caught off his guard, suddenly banked in the hope of being able to outmanoeuvre the Briton; but it was a forlorn hope. A steady stream of bullets poured into the Fokker, and Immelmann, wounded and incapacitated, could make no effort to right the Fokker, which turned clean over on its right side and fell like a stone to the ground, where it burst into flames.

Immelmann had fought his last fight, had brought down his last foe. Yet even as the German went hurtling to his death, the second Fokker swung round, with the evident intention of getting at M'Cubbin before he could right his F.E. But M'Cubbin was ready, for as he saw Immelmann go slithering down to earth he banked sharply, turned in an amazingly short circle, and made direct for the Fokker. The gallant Lieutenant knew all about Fokkers and their disadvantages, even as he knew the advantages they possessed if once their pilots could obtain the right position. The Fokker has such a short span of wing that it cannot be banked to any great extent without developing a nose-dive, so that at the end of a dive it has to make a large circle. The F.E., on the other hand, having a much wider span, can practically "stand on its wing tips," which enables it to turn in an exceedingly narrow circle.

In just the same way that naval men have worked out sea-tactics, so have our airmen evolved air-tactics, and M'Cubbin was an adept. He knew perfectly the capabilities of his F.E., and as the Fokker reached the end of its dive and began the wide swooping circle. Lieutenant M'Cubbin steered his machine into what may be termed the centre of that circle. By steep banks and sudden turns he kept his machine inside, while his observer was slipping in fresh cartridges, merely waiting for the exact moment to come when he could fire.

Then the unexpected happened: the pilot of the Fokker, evidently nervous of a man who could outclass Immelmann, and realizing that M'Cubbin's F.E. had the advantage in powers plus that of position, instead of completing the circle which might have brought him to where he could attack, suddenly gave up the fight, and went sailing away to friendly shelter, leaving M'Cubbin the victor in what had been a thrilling battle!

M'Cubbin and his observer were both uninjured, but their machine bore honourable marks of the fight, its planes being holed in numerous places, and its fuselage looking like the top of a pepper-box.

A week later M'Cubbin fought another battle, and was not so fortunate, although he was almost as successful. In many respects this second battle had in it more of the elements that thrill than that with Immelmann, although because of the lauded prowess of the German more glamour surrounded the previous affair.

Lieutenant M'Cubbin with four other machines had been on a bombing expedition, and, their work completed, the airmen were returning home when a Fokker followed them and attacked one of the British machines. M'Cubbin was well in advance, but, looking round, saw the Fokker coming; so banking, he swung round, recrossed our lines, and sailed into the M'Cubbin fight.

M'Cubbin used all his skill to obtain the advantage of position, and the Fokker pilot did his best to get above his foe and use the tactics which had always proved so successful. While the aeroplanes were engaged in lighting for position, the machine-guns spat angrily, bullets spattered through nacelles and ripped their way through the planes. Almost simultaneously two bullets got home: one from the British battle-plane hit the Fokker, which toppled over and hurtled to destruction; the other, from the Fokker, smashed its way through the nacelle, entered M'Cubbin's shoulder, passed clean through the muscles, and lodged in his forearm.

By a supreme effort M'Cubbin kept his head; the pain was terrible, and the arm was rendered utterly useless; blood flowed freely, weakening him every minute. But to descend then meant falling into the enemy's hands, and M'Cubbin was determined that that should not happen if it were humanly possible to avoid doing so. He swung his machine round and, his eyes misty, his head swimming, he made a bolt for his own base. Over the trenches filled with British soldiers, who had breathlessly watched the combat in mid-air, and had cheered enthusiastically when they saw the Fokker go down; over the trenches and beyond to where the aerodrome stood clearly marked out, M'Cubbin drove his aerial steed. Every moment seemed an age, every necessary touch of the 'joy-stick' jolted the wounded arm; but M'Cubbin held on, knowing that he must get his machine to safety quickly lest the petrol ran out owing to the tank having been shot through. Onward and downward, in a beautiful volplane he went to meet the uprising ground, coming to rest as lightly as a bird, and then collapsing through loss of blood the moment his machine touched earth. For his gallant conduct in these two encounters Lieutenant M'Cubbin received the D.S.O.

CHAPTER 14

Some Zeppelin Strafers

On the night of March 31st-April 1st, 1916, three Zeppelins sailed over the stormy wastes of the North Sea, reached the East Coast, and then separated, each to carry out the fell work assigned to it by those safe in far-off Germany. One of them, L15, in charge of Commander Breithaupt, headed for the Metropolis. Breithaupt, who had received the Iron Cross and the *Order pour le Mérite* for a previous raid on London in September 1915, profiting by the knowledge gained on that occasion, set a course which he hoped would enable him to elude certain batteries of the land defences. His guide was Father Thames, and he steered his giant gas-bag so skilfully that he penetrated some considerable distance inland before he was discovered. Probably he and his crew were congratulating themselves upon their feat, and expecting to be able to reach their objective before being discovered. They were, however, sadly disillusioned. Suddenly the inky darkness was pierced by two brilliant shafts of light which shot up and, with unerring aim, swathed the Zeppelin in a white effulgence which dazzled the crew.

Realizing that searchlights were the prelude to shrapnel, Breithaupt immediately took action. He released the bombs intended for London Town in order to lighten his craft and enable him to rise quickly out of range of the searchlights, and especially of the anti-aircraft guns which he knew would presently open fire.

Even as the first bomb crashed thunderously below, there came another sound from the earth, and a shell, followed quickly by others, went screaming up past the Zeppelin. A circle of bursting stars seemed to be made round the doomed airship, and one of them burst right on top of the envelope, near the tail, making a great hole in the fabric and causing the gas to escape in large quantities. The Zeppelin, despite the fact that her crew frantically loosed most of her bombs, began to fall. As she slowly descended, yet another shell caught her, and Breithaupt, realizing that he was in sore straits, swung his monstrous craft round and tried to head her northward. If he hoped to give the slip to the searchlights, he was grievously disappointed, for the pencils of light seemed glued on to L15, never leaving her for a single second; and the batteries maintained a terrific fire. The marksmanship on that night was remarkably good, for yet another shell smashed one if not two of the propellers of the Zeppelin, and the watchers below saw that she was now pursuing an erratic course, evidently being quite out of control.

Meanwhile, ranging over the eastern counties, another raider was finding things rather uncomfortable. Her commander had endeavoured to elude the outer defences of London, but, unfortunately for him, the airship had been 'spotted' and very soon was under heavy bombardment from the batteries beneath. At the same time, above the roar of the airship's engines there came to her commander a sound which told him that not only had he land defences threatening him, but that an aeroplane was also buzzing around!

The pilot of this particular 'plane was Second-Lieutenant A. de Bath Brandon, a young New Zealander who had taken his 'ticket' only a brief three weeks before, and was totally inexperienced in aerial fighting. The Germans, however, were to discover that British airmen are daring enough for anything; for Lieutenant Brandon, who had ascended from his station immediately news of the raiders had been received, catching sight of the Zeppelin flying 3000 feet above, steered boldly to the attack.

Now, it takes an aeroplane some minutes to climb 3000 feet, and in the meantime the pilot knew that it was not at all unlikely that the Zeppelin might jettison its cargo of bombs and, thus lightened, be able to escape scot-free. Lieutenant Brandon determined that this should not be; so, getting every ounce of power from his engine, and setting his machine to climb at her fastest, he rose higher and higher, until at last he was directly over the gas-bag. On the top of the envelope some of the Zeppelin crew were ready for him with their machine-guns, while the airship's searchlights were sweeping the darkness in an effort to pick up the daring wasp that was so foolhardy as to attack the giant of the air.

Lieutenant Brandon, as soon as he was in position favourable to attack, let loose several bombs, some of which went whizzing past the envelope, while one at least struck home, but with what effect was uncertain.

What happened after that is not clear; but later that same night Lieutenant Brandon was engaged in another attack on a Zeppelin, and gave her the benefit of a couple more bombs, hitting her on the nose. It seems not at all unlikely that L15 which, as we have seen, had received a nasty mauling from the anti-aircraft batteries, was the identical Zeppelin which felt the force of these latter bombs. This much is certain, however: when day broke, L15 was discovered by the steam trawler *Olivine* (Lieutenant-Commander W. R. Mackintosh, R.N.R.) floating near the Knock Lightship with her back broken. Breithaupt and his crew surrendered, but not before they had taken the precaution of placing a time-bomb which destroyed the airship while her captors were attempting to tow her into harbour.

It is significant of the German attitude in war, and of the kind of treatment that the Huns expect as a just recompense for their brutal crimes, that the prisoners were not a little surprised at the humane treatment they received! Commander Breithaupt, indeed, as though to palliate the crime of his crew, took upon himself all responsibility, saying that his men simply obeyed orders.

It has taken the Germans a long time to realize that Britons fight with clean hands, even against a foe who does not hesitate to use every means, foul or fair, in the pursuit of his villainous designs.

For his fine feat, Lieutenant Brandon received the D.S.O.

Following this raid, there were a number of other visits over various English counties by hostile airships; but we have no space to recount all the heroic deeds performed by British airmen in driving off the raiders. A few incidents may, however, be recounted, as, for instance, the gallant attacks made by Flight-Lieutenants Vincent Nicholl, F. G. Darby Hards, and C. H. C. Smith, all of the Royal Naval Air Service.

On April 25th, 1916, an unknown number of airships visited Essex and Kent and, without having committed any damage, were returning to their base, when they were attacked by our airmen. Flight-Lieutnants Nicholl and Hards pursued one of them for sixty miles out to sea. Coming up with her they dived until they were within a few hundred feet of the airship, when they attacked her with darts and bombs, with what result did not transpire. Flight-Lieutenant Smith, also, chased another of the Zeppelins for fifty miles, hanging on to her relentlessly until it was useless to proceed any farther. He was returning to his base when he sighted a fleet of enemy warships accompanied by submarines. Naval airmen are ready for anything that ploughs the seas or sails through the air, and Lieutenant Smith promptly attacked the submarines, dropping his bombs with such accuracy that the undersea-craft were very glad to clang down their hatches and submerge, without waiting for the gallant aviator to repeat the dose.

On July 31st other raiders appeared, and on this occasion scattered bombs over a wide area, but doing little material damage and fortunately without inflicting any casualties. It was during this raid that one of our aeroplanes, piloted by an officer whose name was not given, pursued a Zeppelin for thirty miles out to sea, and on coming within range attacked her with his machine-gun. Then hard luck came to him, for while he was still pulling the trigger of his gun the weapon broke and a portion of it crashed into him, stunning him so badly that for a while he was unable to control his machine, which began to drop. The rush of the cool air revived the gallant aviator, however, while the machine was still well above the water, and he succeeded in regaining control of it; but of the enemy he had hoped to 'strafe' there was no sign. He was therefore compelled to return to his station, feeling, no doubt, pretty sore at the scurvy trick that Fate had played him.

In another chapter we have told the story of the brilliant way in which Lieutenant Warneford destroyed a Zeppelin in flight, and this performance was repeated over British soil by Lieutenant W. L. Robinson on September 3rd, 1916. The moment was indeed a dramatic one, for this was the first aerial monster to be brought down in England, and the hundreds of thousands of people who witnessed the thrilling deed were fired with a righteous emotion born of their knowledge that the victim was engaged upon a dastardly attempt to murder their loved ones.

On September 5th, 1916, the *London Gazette* published the following announcement:

> H.M. the King has been graciously pleased to award the V.C. to the undermentioned officer:
> Lieutenant Wm. Leefe Robinson (Worcester Regt. and R.F.C.), for most conspicuous bravery.
> He attacked an enemy airship under circumstances of great difficulty and danger, and sent it crashing to the ground as a flaming wreck.
> He had been in the air for more than two hours, and had previously attacked another airship during his flight.

The Destruction of a Zeppelin at Cuffley by Lieut. Robinson

That is the bald official announcement, which goes into no details, and very wisely, because the enemy would give much to know the means whereby that airship and others which later met the same doom were destroyed. It is possible, however, to fill in a few items of interest which may tend to increase the admiration of British people for the man whom so many of them regard as their deliverer.

Of the lieutenant himself it may be said that he was born at Tellidetta, South Coorg, South India, and had not turned twenty-one when he won his Victoria Cross. His father was Mr Horace Robinson, son of Mr W. C. Robinson, R.N., Chief Naval Constructor at Portsmouth Dockyard. The hero of the great raid was brought to England when he was six months old, but returned to India when he was seven years. At fourteen he was back in England, at St Bees School, Cumberland, later going to France and eventually entering Sandhurst. That was in August 1914, just after the war broke out, and on December 16th of that year he was gazetted to the Worcestershire Regiment.

Joining the Flying Corps soon afterward, he was in France as an observer from February 1915 to May 9th, on which date he was wounded in the arm by shrapnel while flying over Lille. Returning to England, after convalescence he went into training as a pilot, and took his 'ticket' on July 28th, 1915. Making a speciality of night flying, he saw much service and performed good work in connexion with the air-raids over England during the seven months preceding that 'one crowded hour of glorious life' when he brought down the giant foe. Seven months later, during the strenuous fighting which prepared the way for the great British advance beyond Arras, and which grew to proportions greater than those of any previous battles in the air, he developed motor trouble during a combat with the German champion Festner, and was forced to descend behind the enemy lines, where he was captured by a number of German soldiers.

So much for the man. Now for the details of his heroic deed.

On September 2nd, 1916, Zeppelins came over to England in force, and an official report placed their number at thirteen and announced that the raid was the most formidable Zeppelin attack which had been made on Great Britain. Unfortunately for the raiders, they paid their visit just after the lighting precautions of London and certain other areas had been improved, and also at about the time when the defence organization generally had been perfected. The result of the new lighting arrangements was that the airships, "instead of steering a steady course as in the raids of the spring and last autumn, groped about in the darkness looking for a safe avenue of approach to their objectives."

With the airships which directed their attentions to the more eastern counties we are not concerned here, our main interest being connected with one of the three which were able to approach within reach of London. The first inkling that the people of the Metropolis and the surrounding district had of the presence of the raider was the crash of exploding bombs and the barking of the anti-aircraft guns. Where the bombs were failing the people wisely kept within doors, remaining as calm as could be expected under such circumstances; but farther away spectators were to be found everywhere, peering up into the sky, and following the pencil lines of light at the ends of which the form of the airship was to be seen clearly outlined. The bursting shells made the sky beautiful, and many a cry and shout went up that the raider was hit. Then after a while there came a wonderful stillness, and the people of London stood waiting, spellbound, as though expecting something novel and tremendous to happen.

They were not disappointed. The lines of light seemed to have become immovably focused upon the airship. A silence that seemed to last hours, but which was really only of a few moments' duration, and then the miracle happened: a light spurted along the airship, a light that could be seen for many miles, and yet which was as the feeble flickering of a guttering candle compared with the flare that almost immediately followed. The whole heavens were lighted up by a crimson glow, which made it possible to read—if there had been anyone so nonchalant as to want to read!—even though the hour was between 2 and 3 in the morning. A moment's deathly silence, as though the watching crowds could scarcely realize what had happened, and then up rose such a cheering, such a shouting as surely has seldom been heard; for the people of London at last grasped the fact that someone, they knew not who, had performed a miracle, and had saved many of them from a tragic fate.

Meanwhile, the stricken airship was falling earthward, like a flaming dragon, nose downward. As though her flaming, blazing envelope were acting as a parachute, she fell slowly, and not rapidly as many expected; but she fell, nevertheless, and, as an eyewitness wrote:

> . . . . when yet some 5000 feet up, the light, especially at the lower end, turned to a brilliant ruby, lightening away through crimson and pink to an incandescent white at the top, the fol-

lowing flames, above, being pale yellow.

As the monster came nearer to earth, the spectators in the immediate neighbourhood heard a crackling as of exploding ammunition (the cases of which were later found making a track which indicated the path of the airship's drift); and then, with a final plunge, the raider dived to earth, falling near Hill Farm Cottage, outside Cuffley. Remarkable to relate, the storekeeper in that farm heard nothing! He was sleeping the sleep of the just, surely!

When at last the airship touched earth, and the flames were mounting upward, those who had witnessed the spectacle saw three coloured lights, suspended, as it were, from the dome of heaven itself, and they realized that somewhere up there the men who had braved the machine-guns of the aerial foe were hovering, as though looking down in triumph upon their fallen enemy.

And what had happened up there? How had this great work been done? Someday, perhaps, the world will know the story in its entirety; but, meantime, we must be content with the facts as they were allowed to be given by those who took part in the great achievement. And we cannot do better than round off this story with the accounts of two officers, one of them the man who later was to receive the Victoria Cross for his personal part in the affair.

Lieutenant Robinson soon after the event said:

I had been up something over an hour when I saw the first Zeppelin. She was flying high, and I followed her, climbing to get a position above. But there was a heavy fog, and she escaped me. I attacked her at long range, but she made off before I could see if I had done any damage. The next ship I saw I determined I would attack from the first position I found. I met her just after two o'clock. She was flying 10,000 feet. Soon she appeared to catch fire in her forward petrol tank. The flames spread rapidly along her body. She made off eastward on fire. In several minutes she dipped by the nose and dived slowly in flames to the earth. I was so pleased that in my excitement I pulled the 'joy-stick' and looped the loop several times. Then I showed my signal to stop firing and came back.

Later still, when he was presented with a handsome cheque which had been promised to the airman who should first bring down a German airship over Britain, he made the following modest speech to the enthusiastic company assembled to do him honour:

The thing that I had the good fortune to do is a thing which anybody in the corps, you all know perfectly well, would have done if they had had the same good fortune that I had.

I was not the only one to go up after that Zeppelin. You must know that in the case of every Zeppelin that has been over England or near England there have been many airmen who have gone up, and in far worse conditions than I had, I think, that night—in conditions that meant almost certain death.

Many of them have met their death in chasing these inhuman murderers who have come over here.

Men, friends of mine, have been maimed for life by going up just on the off-chance of 'strafing' them on absolutely impossible nights, nights when it has been exceedingly difficult to land, misty nights, nights when you can't see the ground—you get up into the mists and can see nothing of earth. All these deeds I consider a hundred times more heroic than the thing I did.

It was, I must impress upon you all, merely good fortune on my part. I feel a lot of honour and glory have already been given me, and I feel almost, I would not say criminal; I can't quite express my feelings on the subject, but I know I don't deserve all this kindness—all that you dear people have shown me.

I just want to thank you, and am sorry English is such a poor language. If I could express myself as I could wish I should say a good bit more, but I simply cannot.

One of those other officers, to whom Lieutenant Robinson so handsomely referred, had also a story to tell, which throws a little more light upon the achievement of the hero of the occasion. That particular officer, who must be nameless, had gone up in a high-powered biplane, and had to climb to nearly 10,000 feet before he could engage the raider, which, harassed by two other aeroplanes, was endeavouring to get away, at the same time rapping out a hot fire with its machine-guns. The officer, said:

> The airship was travelling at top speed, first diving, and then ascending, and apparently Lieutenant Robinson, who was the officer piloting the biplane which had first attacked the raider, anticipated the manoeuvre.
>
> The commander of the airship threw out tremendous clouds of black smoke, which completely hid him from our view, and in which he managed to rise. A few seconds later we saw the air-

ship a couple of thousand feet above us, and at the same altitude was Lieutenant Robinson, although a matter of, perhaps, half a mile away. Immediately Robinson headed his machine for the raider, and flying at a terrific speed, it appeared that he was going to charge the monster.

Then followed that brilliant spectacle of the sky, and, as the airship fell in flames, a second aerial monster approached the airmen, who were ready for it. Evidently the sight of the fate of his companion made the commander of this airship decide to hurry off, for he promptly and swiftly turned his craft round and "scurried off as fast as his engines would enable him to travel. At such a height and in the darkness it was impossible to pick him up."

All Britain was heartened by the brilliant achievement of Lieutenant Robinson, for until then there had been a feeling that our successes against raiding aircraft were more the result of good chance than anything else; the Cuffley episode proved that preparedness and skill had been brought to such a pitch that raiders could never again repeat their easy murders of the past.

To tell the stories of the 'strafing' of yet four more Zeppelins during raids on Britain would be to paraphrase the account of the one just given, for in every particular, so far as we are at present allowed to know, the deeds of Second-Lieutenants F. Sowrey and Alfred de Bath Brandon[1] (both of the Royal Flying Corps), when two Zeppelins were brought down on September 24-25, were duplicates of the achievement of Lieutenant Robinson. The Zeppelins were part of a force which visited England on the date named, and one of them, at least, was attacked by Lieutenants Sowrey and Brandon and other airmen, who chased her from the south of London as she headed north and then turned north-east.

The airship, which was L32, was flying higher than any of her predecessors had flown over London. Such little details of the event as were allowed to leak out show that Lieutenant Sowrey, when he had climbed high enough, attacked the Zeppelin and was in turn attacked; the giant ship manoeuvred so that her machine-guns could be brought to bear upon the aviator, who by wonderful skill succeeded in obtaining a position so that, in the manner which is the close secret of the Flying Service, he was able to get in the blow that set the Zep-

---

1. A previous exploit of Lieutenant Brandon's is described at the beginning of this chapter.

pelin on fire from end to end and sent her swiftly to earth, a flaming wreck. The second ship (L33) to meet disaster that night was so badly knocked about by the gunfire of the London defences that, owing to loss of gas, she had to descend near the Essex coast, where the Germans blew up their craft and then marched along the quiet country roads in quest of someone to whom they could surrender. A special constable met them, and they asked him the way to a certain town. One of the party then volunteered the astounding information:

Zeppelin engine exploded—we crew—prisoners of war.

No doubt that 'special' had about the funniest sensation running riot through his body, for naturally he did not know whether they were armed and would turn upon him. British to the backbone, however, he coolly took the twenty odd men under his care and piloted them toward the village post office, being presently joined by other specials, and here the prisoners were inspected. Eventually the whole of the crew were taken into custody by the military and removed to certain barracks.

The attempt on the part of the commander to blow up his airship was only partially successful, so that when the dawn came wondering spectators saw a tangled mass of wreckage close on 700 feet long and over threescore feet and ten in diameter. The uninitiated would have supposed that such a wreck could prove of little use to anyone, but sufficient was left undamaged to enable the authorities to obtain a very fair idea of the construction of what was undoubtedly one of Germany's latest airships.

Thus by gunfire and aeroplane had two more German raiders been accounted for, and, about a week later—on October 1st, to be precise—yet another Zeppelin met a flaming fate within a few miles of the Metropolis.

On the night in question, ten Zeppelins crossed the East Coast, and one of them which had London for her objective was commanded, as it was afterward discovered, by Commander Mathy, a pilot who had previously raided the City of our Empire, and had given an account of his experience to an American newspaper man. Just about midnight this Zeppelin was sighted approaching London, and, with searchlights piercing the skies and revealing her position to the artillerymen below, the defences of the Metropolis vigorously opened fire upon her. Hundreds of thousands of people were watching the spectacle, and saw what they naturally did not understand at first. Shells from the anti-aircraft guns were throwing up a starry curtain of fire, through which the Zeppelin cither could not pass or dared not for fear of what might happen.

The searchlights were evidently baffling the crew in her, and many attempts were made to escape the white blaze of light focused upon her. For what seemed endless minutes—perhaps it was less than half an hour—the raider was held in the beams; then she eluded them for a brief while, during which the spectators watched open-mouthed, not knowing where she would next appear. With not a little relief they presently saw her again, caught by the searchlights, and once more the artillery boomed, the shells bursting apparently in close proximity to the great envelope.

And then, silence and darkness: the searchlights were shut off, the gunfire ceased. The people of London and the surrounding district held their breath. Recollection of what had happened a few seconds after such a silence on the occasion of the destruction of the raider at Cuffley came to the thousands who had been in the streets on that historic night, and men, women, and children waited with bated breath—expectant, hopeful.

They were not disappointed. Suddenly the intense darkness was broken by a curious yellow light, which quickly developed into a crimson blaze, illuminating the country for miles around.

A momentary hovering in midair, and then the airship, flaming from end to end, began to fall, those spectators who were near enough being able to see the white lines of her aluminium framework clear-cut in the reddish flame. Everybody knew what had happened: somewhere up there, while they had been watching and waiting in breathless anticipation, an airman had been at work in some mysterious but effective way; but it was not until sometime later that they knew who the aviator was. His name was Second-Lieutenant Wulstan Joseph Tempest. He had been spending the evening with some friends, and had been called away to meet the invaders. He ascended 10,000 feet and waited in the air for over two hours before the Zeppelin appeared. He promptly attacked, pursuing her until he was within striking range. Then he had struck, and struck home.

Immediately after the Zeppelin caught fire he had travelled the complete length of her, parallel with her all the time. More than once, in order to avoid colliding with the burning mass of his victim, he had to nosedive. Eventually he landed in safety miles away from the place where he had first taken the air, and was driven back to his station in a motor to receive a fine ovation from his comrades. Later he was awarded the D.S.O.

Because it tells, as plainly as may be told, the nature of the experience of an aviator in his fight with a Zeppelin, an airman's account—it refers to the earlier days of aerial fighting—published in the *Pall Mall Gazette* may be quoted here.

> The pilot of the aeroplane has an instinctive feeling that a Zeppelin is somewhere near him. He cannot hear because of the noise of his own engine, and he cannot see because of the intensity of the darkness all around him. His feeling is soon confirmed when he finds himself the focus of two, three, four, or more searchlights, and the anti-aircraft guns commence to fire. This is another deadly danger he has to contend with: there is as much chance, sometimes more, of our own anti-aircraft shells hitting him instead of the raiding airship.
>
> By means of his wireless key, however, he is able to communicate with his aerodrome, who immediately telephone to the guns to cease fire, but during the time that must necessarily elapse before this comes to pass he is in very grave danger. More so even than the airship, for one direct hit would not, in all probability, be sufficient to bring down an airship, but most certainly would destroy a frail and tiny aeroplane.
>
> The combat between the aeroplane and the Zeppelin might be compared to that between a British destroyer and the German Dreadnoughts in the recent Jutland battle. Dashing in with great rapidity and skill, the tiny one-gunned aeroplane fires its broadside, then makes off as fast as possible to get out of range of the comparatively heavy-armed airship. From thence onward it develops into a fight for the upper position, for once above the Zeppelin the aeroplane pilot can use his bombs,[2] and the broad back of the gas-bag offers a target which can hardly be missed.
>
> Again, some Zeppelins are not armed, as were the very earliest fighting craft, with a machine-gun above the envelope; thus the aeroplane has the Zepp at his mercy, and is out of danger himself. Should he be unable to climb above, the only other vulnerable spot is the stern; the airship machine-guns fire only

---

2. This was the method of attack followed by Warneford and some other of the earlier fighters with Zeppelins.

fore and amidships, and cannot fire aft.

In manoeuvring, the aeroplane has the great advantage of being remarkably quick in turning, climbing, and coming down. The Zeppelin, again, is very susceptible to flame and explosion of any kind; the gas in the envelope, a mixture of hydrogen and air, forms an extremely explosive mixture. The aeroplane, owing to the fabric of which it is composed, and the petrol needed for propulsion, is to a certain degree inflammable, but not nearly to the same extent as the airship. *Per contra*, the airship possesses a distinct advantage in that it is able to shut off its engines, and to hover, which it is impossible for an aeroplane to do. Again, in the matter of speed in a forward direction, and, for that matter, backward also—for the Zeppelin's engines are reversible—the aeroplane holds the palm with an average speed of sixty miles per hour, to the airship's fifty.

The combat finished, the aeroplane pilot has yet to make a landing, surely the most dangerous and tricky manoeuvre of the whole fight. The difficulties and dangers thus encountered are too obvious to need explanation, further than to say that the landing has to be effected in the dark, with only a blinding, dazzling electric ground-light for guidance.

Commander Mathy, the pilot who met his doom in the raid of October 1st, told a reporter, amongst other things, that he was not afraid of aeroplanes. "I think I could make it interesting for them, unless there was a regular swarm." Well, Commander Mathy had things made interesting for him, and the continued destruction of Zeppelins when they have ventured over Britain is proof that those who have charge of the defences are not sitting twiddling their thumbs. No means of solving the problem have been left untried, no precautions have been neglected, as a batch of raiders discovered on November 27th, 1916, after a pause of some weeks in their activities. On that night a number of airships approached the North-East Coast, most carefully avoiding London, under the impression, no doubt, that by giving the Metropolis a wide berth they would be outside the range of effective defences.

They were disillusioned, however, and found that not only around London but also in other parts of the country there was danger for raiders.

Four of the five airships which took part in the raid attacked the

North-East Coast, dropping bombs on Durham and Yorkshire, luckily with but little damage to life and property. In exactly the same way as Lieutenants Robinson and Tempest had attacked their aerial foes, one of their comrades of the Royal Flying Corps—Lieutenant I.V. Pyott—drove into action with a raider on that November night. There was a short but none the less stern fight between the wasp and the hawk, and then the London scenes were re-enacted: the great airship caught fire, the flames spread through its whole length, and the blazing mass fell into the sea while the night watchers shouted themselves hoarse.

Boats were hastily put out to see if there were any survivors, but nothing was seen of the destroyed craft, not even when morning came: all that betokened the great event was a thick film of oil upon the surface of the waters.

While Lieutenant Pyott was engaged pushing home his attack, away down the coast other intrepid airmen were busy. The fifth airship had struck inland toward the Midlands, where she dropped several bombs. The raider, however, was destined not to escape. As she turned about and made off for the coast the batteries bombarded her, aeroplanes pursued her, and she was apparently so severely mauled that she had to come to a standstill near the Norfolk coast to effect temporary repairs. When the grey fingers of the dawn began to creep into the eastern sky she was plainly visible, and was noticed to be travelling eastward, at a great height, with several Royal Naval Air Service machines in her wake. The fact that it was growing light gave the crew of this Zeppelin advantages which the raiders over London had not possessed, for the former could easily see the intrepid attackers approaching and turn machine-guns upon them. The aviators were not to be discouraged, however, and the people lining the coast were given an exhibition of aerial fighting at a height of 8000 feet.

It was a fight worth watching, too. Down below an armed trawler was bombarding the discomfited raider as she tried to shake off her persistent foes, who were firing at her as rapidly as possible. Three of the airmen—Lieutenant Egbert Cadbury and Sub-Lieutenants E. L. Pulling and G. W. R. Fane—drove in as closely as possible, sweeping past the Zeppelin's machine-guns, rising above her, swooping down and performing amazing evolutions around her, all the time firing vigorously, and hitting her repeatedly, until at last the giant envelope caught fire, the flames roared their way along her whole length, and she went plunging into the sea.

RAIDING THE RAIDER OUR GIANT SEAPLANES TAKING THE AIR TO CUT OFF A ZEPPELIN'S RETREAT

CHAPTER 15

On Fire!

Sitting in the trenches which scar the once fair fields of Flanders, British Tommies have seen the great flying battle in progress thousands of times, and probably few of these men of the trenches, who live in the hell of high explosive and shrapnel, would willingly change places with the bird-men. One sight alone is sufficient to make the strongest-nerved watcher shiver—the sight of an aeroplane falling a flaming mass through the air, carrying, probably two men, certainly one, to what seems to be an awful death.

Here is a story of such a spectacle—one only of hundreds that have been vouchsafed to men who never want to witness the thrilling drama again.

Away back in June 1915 (to be exact, Friday the 18th), one of our machines, driven by Second-Lieutenant W. H. Dyke Acland (Royal Devon Yeomanry and R.F.C.) accompanied by an officer observer, was reconnoitring over Poelcappelle at a height of 4000 feet, when a large German aeroplane approached, and thundering in close proximity began to attack. Now, that German machine was no adversary to be treated lightly: it was double-engined, had two propellers and a double fuselage, and could work up a speed which enabled it to make rings round our machine. This it promptly did, loosing a hurricane of machine-gun bullets as it did so, although, apparently, without inflicting any damage upon the British aeroplane, thanks to the brilliant way in which Lieutenant Dyke Acland handled his mount.

The 'scrap' took place at a range of about 200 yards; and after the Germans had thus fruitlessly squandered their ammunition, Dyke Acland's companion, who had been waiting for the opportune moment, ripped in about fifty rounds from his machine-gun, several of which apparently got home, for immediately afterward the German machine began to waver in its headlong course, the roar of its engines ceased, the aeroplane gave a nasty tilt, and then tipped its nose downward. For a sheer 2000 feet that monster 'plane nosedived, seemingly out of control, and Lieutenant Acland and his observer were not a little 'bucked' at the thought that they had so successfully tackled their big antagonist. Their delight subsided somewhat when presently they saw the German machine flatten out somewhere about half a mile below them, and then begin to stagger along, flying slowly and erratically, evidently just able to keep an even keel for sufficient time to enable it to get to safety.

As the Britishers had a certain object in view, which was to reconnoitre German positions, they made no attempt to finish off their enemy, although it seemed a shame to leave a job uncompleted. However, they had done remarkably well to have scared the German away, and were free to go ahead with their immediate work, which they promptly did.

But, alas, what the German aeroplane had been unable to accomplish, German anti-aircraft guns succeeded in doing; for while Lieutenant Dyke Acland was steering his machine, a big shell *whoofed* up into the air, burst with a nasty crash, and sent out a multitude of singing bullets which tore holes in the planes and perforated the petrol tank. As the job was almost finished, the airmen decided that, in view of the precious information they had obtained, it was better to wing homeward than to wait for another of those unpleasant messengers of death. They were, moreover, in an exceedingly critical condition, because the petrol leaking from the tank had caught fire. In such circumstances, it does not take long for control wires to be burnt away or for the tail of the machine to be caught by the flames. The consequences were too awful to contemplate; and men who had seen aeroplanes slip through space like burning torches had no pressing desire to be the occupants of a machine presenting such a spectacle to a jubilant enemy.

So Lieutenant Acland promptly stood his machine on its nose and dived for the earth. The result was that the petrol, instead of running back toward the engine, began to run down the front of the body, the roaring lire gathering in intensity as the machine slipped through space, so that in a very few seconds the aeroplane was enveloped in flames.

From below it must have been a thrilling spectacle. To those in the machine it was a horrifying experience. The fire licked round their legs, burning them badly; the heat cracked the glass in the pilot's goggles and burnt away the surrounding fabric; but, although suffering severely, the lieutenant stuck to his seat, resisting, as did his observer, the temptation to which some men have succumbed: to risk all in a leap from what might easily prove to be a cremating furnace! Down, down, the machine dropped, not erratically, but steadily in answer to the touch of the cool-headed yet scorching pilot; while to add to the terrors of the moment, the rounds of ammunition which had not been pumped into the big German aeroplane went off in a rattle, accompanied by the *popping* of the cartridges in the pilot's revolver!

To those who watched, and to those who were watched, it seemed as though the downward journey would never end, or, if it did, that the passengers would be incinerated. Long before the machine reached the ground a good part of its framework was burnt, and the remainder was blazing; at any second the tail might simply drop off. The blades of the propeller, made of hard wood, were "so much burnt that the propeller ceased to revolve in the rush of air."

Mother Earth was reached at long last, a perfect landing was made, and the aviators, scarcely believing in their good fortune, leaped out of the furnace: as they did so, the tail of the machine dropped off; while Lieutenant Dyke Acland, as though he had not suffered sufficiently already, tripped over a wire stay, fell, and sprained his knee! Fortunately he had been able, by his plucky coolness, to bring his wrecked machine into the British lines; otherwise, both he and his observer would have been taken prisoner. As it was, the German guns out yonder blazed away at them with shrapnel while willing hands were collecting those parts of the machine which could be utilized again.

Badly burnt as he was (although he had fortunately not received any fatal injury) Lieutenant Dyke Acland, before he would go into hospital, calmly sat down and wrote out his report, winding up with a brief account of the flaming descent, and summing up his impressions in the laconic sentence: "The whole of the nacelle seemed to be in flames." Then, because it might be needed by some keeper of the records, he gave geographical details of the spot where he had landed!

For his magnificent courage and devotion to duty, Lieutenant Dyke Acland had bestowed upon him the Order of St George by the Tsar of Russia.

CHAPTER 16

The Battle of Seventy Aeroplanes

When, before the war, artistic prophets dared to depict squadrons of aeroplanes fighting in midair, most of us poured scorn on their predictions. We were most of us content to believe that there might, 'in the next war,' be occasional duels between two rival machines with the whole space of the heavens to manoeuvre in; but the greater thing was declared to be utterly impossible, because, it was explained, men scarcely knew how to handle an aeroplane in a 'joy trip,' let alone pilot one in the midst of dozens of other machines with their guns all firing as rapidly as their marksmen could feed them with cartridges. As a matter of fact, many months of the Great War had passed before the rival aerial fleets had arrived at a degree of efficiency to warrant such tactics; but those who believed in the possibilities of the new fighting arm had little doubt that the day would come when, even as squadrons of cruisers can manoeuvre in the waters, so aeroplanes would go forth in squadrons and engage their rivals.

Stage by stage, the new method of warfare evolved on experimental lines. The single scouter took to itself a companion; the two grew into several, some of them to act merely as scouts, but others battle-planes, designed and armed to fight the strongest hostile machines; until, in November 1916—nearly twenty-eight months after the opening of the Great War—there came the first great crash between rival air-squadrons in large force.

The Allies had won the ascendancy of the air, and their airmen were incessantly winging their way over the German lines, scouting, observing, bombing, fighting, patrolling and driving back the would-be aerial raiders. The Germans, utterly outclassed, scarcely dared take the air for some time; and then came a renewal of activity on their part. The Somme battle had been fought and won, and away in the rear the Germans were busy making fresh fortifications which were, so they boasted, to hold up any further 'push' that the Allies might try to make. Naturally, the German soldiers labouring at their gigantic task—the like of which had never been undertaken in warfare before—were not allowed much peace. Allied aeroplanes constantly sped overhead, bombing whatever was worth bombing, and at last this incessant annoyance roused the Germans to action. Once again their airmen went aloft, in force this time, to try to put an end to the pestering of their foes.

The crash came on November 9th, and it came over the German lines, in the direction of Vaulx-Vraucourt, to the north-east of Bapaume, that strategically important point in the curved German front. With the military depots at Vaulx-Vraucourt as their objective, a number of our bombing machines, escorted by several battle-planes, totalling thirty in all, set off in a formation which had been proved effective, some flying higher than the others and with fighting 'planes covering the bombers at all points to prevent enemy machines from attacking the less formidable 'planes.

They had gone some distance, and were just outside Vaulx-Vraucourt, when the escort sighted a squadron of German fighting machines already in the air. They too were in formation for attack, and were, moreover, in superior numbers, there being probably forty of them. They were barring the way to the place where the bombers were to deposit their devastating loads. That being so, the tricolour-marked battle-planes let their engines all out and swept forward to the combat, which they were determined should take place as near their objective as possible, so that when it was all over the bomb-carriers would not have far to go to accomplish their task.

There was a strong westerly wind blowing at the time, which aided the Allies in the beginning, but was no friend to some later on; for those of our machines which were winged during the conflict were carried in their descent farther over the German positions.

It goes without saying that aerial combats are matters of seconds almost. There is no time for leisurely decision, leisurely movements; everything is done, if it is done at all, at the rush; and in that fashion the raiding machines went to meet their foes.

As soon as they judged they were in range, each pilot engaged the enemy which he had selected—some of them, of course, had more than one to contend against—and there followed such a battle royal as the world had never known before.

Such a large number of aeroplanes, of various types, engaged in a fight to the death at an average height of 5000 feet, makes an impressive sight. To those who are watching below, some look like balls of gold as the sun catches them; others, like big, black birds of prey swooping to the attack of smaller fry, which latter, speedier than the birds of the air, roar defiantly as they drive to an encounter which may spell destruction. Neither the artist's brush nor the writer's pen can paint that picture as it should be painted, and the imagination of the man who has not looked upon such a scene reels at the very idea of it.

Those of our machines which were above the Germans swooped down upon them, firing as they went, while the Teutons, with the wicked-looking muzzles of their machine-guns pointing upward, spat hundreds of bullets at them as they came. It is impossible to follow in detail the twenty minutes' fight, seeing that it was mostly a series of isolated actions—one can but give a general idea of it. Our two-gunned machines simultaneously tackled circling Germans, dived down like hawks, spitting fire as they went, slithered, as it were, down over the planes of German machines as the latter banked and turned and tried to slip away underneath to come up behind their downsweeping foes. How many men looped the loop that day in order to save their lives or in order to come round to position for effective attack none can say. As fast as one German 'plane was driven off and down, another would roar to the attack; and the noise of the battle was as the noise of an engineering shop in which all the plant had run out of gear!

Think of it: seventy engines droning madly—seventy propellers humming till the air seems filled with super-bees—while scores of machine-guns, pitched, as it were, in different keys, are rattling out their discordant songs of hate! And picture it: great winging birds of man's make darting and whirling in majestic swoops, circling with graceful ease—while ever and anon one goes tumbling to earth like a shot pheasant—and, still more awful sight, shot-drilled tanks let their petrol flow and a machine catches fire and dives down a flaming mass, as though some fabled monster striving to storm the gates of Heaven had been struck by the fire of the gods!

In the midst of that battle of the kings of the air, many were the thrilling escapes from sudden death. Here, for instance, is a biplane rushing toward an enemy travelling at terrific speed in the opposite direction; it is a moment filled with horrific possibilities, not merely because both machines have a grim-faced man sitting with his hand clutching the trigger of a gun which can spit out hundreds of deaths a minute, but because the difference of a fraction of an inch in the downward push or the upward pull of a 'joy-stick,' or the slightest overthrust to right or left, may result in a splintering, pounding crash as the two machines meet in a collision which will end in both going headlong to the earth below. Another aeroplane, diving to the attack, may—who knows?—be caught between the on-rushing machines, and the disaster be more terrible still. The margin between life and death is extremely small in such circumstances, and a man needs a cool head and a quick brain!

Not merely one storm of the death-hail, but scores, were breaking in fury, and machines not immediately engaged caught some of the bullets as they missed their real objective and went speeding through the air. Stray bullets were indeed a danger in that battle, if ever they were! And yet, the airmen did not worry about them: each man sought his opponent and fought him until he had driven him off, or perhaps, until some other enemy swooped for his tail from above or, coming up below, raked the full length of his machine with bullets.

A very whirlwind of a fight! Here and there machines darted to and fro, first tackling this foe and then that, banking with startling suddenness and amazing skill, turning in apparent frenzied haste to outmanoeuvre a rival, only to come up against yet another who must be tackled before the enemy who had been given the slip could come up again!

In such fashion did this battle of the air rage; but at last it was over, and those of the Germans who had their machines under control were pelting for safety, leaving the conquerors of the air to go about their business. No fewer than six of the enemy machines had been driven down, most of them out of control, and in one at least the pilot was sagging limp and lifeless in his seat; while of those others which flew away, their formation utterly broken, who can say how many were able again to take the air, or who knows how many of their crew went back uninjured? These things are hidden somewhere in the records of the German Flying Corps, grim reminders of the first great aerial battle.

As for our own casualties, four machines were lost to us, because, being winged, and at the mercy of the westerly wind, they had to descend at the nearest spot and were captured by the Germans. One of the returning aeroplanes was the funeral chariot of a dead observer, and two others were the ambulances of their pilots, who, wounded though they were, piloted their machines against the driving wind, bringing them eventually to their desired haven. But the victorious warriors did not return home until they had sailed on past the scene of their triumph, and their bombers had planted their explosives on the munition dumps and supply-depots at Vaulx-Vraucourt. Thus the enemy's attempt to drive off the attackers had proved a costly failure.

CHAPTER 17

On Patrol

A wind that whistled between the planes, strummed like a harper upon struts and wiring, and drove sheets of water into the aviator, as he sped in the teeth of the storm—such was the accompaniment to one of the fine feats of Captain R. H. G. Neville (Duke of Cornwall's Light Infantry and R.F.C.), a member of the air patrol between British and enemy trenches.

The captain's work was to scare off any enemy machines, or, if they were not to be scared off, then to fight them off; in any case, they were not to be permitted to get behind the British lines and fix prying eyes upon what was being done there.

On this particular day in the latter part of 1916, Captain Neville, who was one of our most skilful pilots, found his task exceedingly difficult. To remain up in such a stormy wind was in itself no easy achievement: add to that the constant vigil necessary in case some daring foe should manage to slip past the patrol, and you have all the elements of a most exciting experience! Despite the fact that he was wrapped up to the very top of his head, with only his eyes showing through his goggles. Captain Neville was by no means so comfortable physically as he could wish; and without doubt the lonely, uninteresting patrol was just a little monotonous—until the droning of the engine, striving, as it were, to outdo the noise of the storm, was broken by what seemed to be a hurricane of sound. A quick glance showed Captain Neville something which almost took away his breath: plunging out of the storm was a big enemy 'plane, which had succeeded in getting quite close before being seen.

For a moment it seemed to Captain Neville that the end of all things had come, because when he sighted the enemy the two machines were so close that it appeared impossible to avoid a collision, and the strength of the storm caused the captain to fear that his machine might not answer quickly enough to the touch on the levers.

Captain Neville gave his controls a jerk which made the aeroplane shiver from end to end; the machine banked steeply, and standing at a dangerous angle, drove round—and as it did so, the enemy aeroplane swept by, the planes of it barely missing the British machine.

And then, before his opponent could grasp what was in the mind of the Britisher, the latter had completed the circle and, coming back, was opening out at the enemy machine. Captain Neville had the advantage of position, and raked the foe fore and aft so plentifully and with such accuracy that his opponent, finding he had entirely lost the advantage of surprise, turned and, giving up all hope of crossing the British lines, made off toward his own.

Then began a stern chase. Captain Neville, when he saw the enemy turn tail, realized that he was probably suffering badly from 'cold feet,' and he resolved to pursue him to the bitter end. Out and away from the British lines, the enemy tore through the rain; after him went the Captain, hanging grimly just behind his tail, like some vengeful bird relentless in pursuit of a monster foe. Showing grey through the driving rain, the earth seemed to be receding at a terrific rate. Although he could see but little, Captain Neville was quickly notified when he was over the German lines; for the appearance of the two machines scudding along, the aeroplane marked with the tricoloured target chasing the one with the black cross, showed the men at the 'Archies' that one of their own kin was in danger. They immediately opened fire at the British machine, and the *rat-tat-tatting* of Captain Neville's Lewis gun was drowned by the crash of bursting shells.

In spite of the shells the captain still held on—held on like grim death; and though he tried every device, the enemy could not shake him off. Captain Neville was running a dreadful gauntlet of fire, and many a gun which had almost found the ever-changing range, narrowly missed bringing the chase to a sudden end. The enemy fled over batteries with whose position he was conversant, in the hope that the pursuer might be hit and brought down in flames; but the Britisher flinched from nothing, and seemed to be invulnerable! On and on through the never-ceasing storm, far over the German lines, until at last Captain Neville realized that his quarry was gliding for earth. That meant one of several things: the enemy's petrol had given out; or perhaps he was nearing his home aerodrome; or again, it might be that he was utterly scared and was going down, taking all chance where he landed.

As the scenery below grew more distinct, Captain Neville saw that the second of these conjectures was the correct one; for presently there loomed the hangars of an aerodrome, toward which the foe was frantically making. The British pilot now called upon his engine for every ounce of power, as he was determined to bring his quarry to bay; and after a few anxious moments caused by the guns below, he succeeded in doing so. He went into the attack with a vehemence that startled the German, who, finding that at last he must fight, replied ineffectually to the fire of his rival; and eventually Captain Neville, by a sharp manoeuvre, obtained the advantage of position, from which he emptied a belt of cartridges into his opponent, whose, machine was so badly mauled that it began to drop. The captain, following it down as far as it was discreet to do, had the gratification of seeing it crash to earth, half a mile from its aerodrome. The chase had not been in vain, and for this and much other fine work on patrol. Captain Neville received his Military Cross.

Here is a brief story, but one which contains heroism and drama as full-blooded as many a longer one.

Captain Dixon (Yorks LT. and R.F.C.), scouring the air on what may be called offensive patrol, adopted tactics with which he completely hoodwinked a certain German airman who fell into a most distressing trap. The gallant captain, whose task was to keep the enemy from getting over the British lines, instead of going for this particular Hun in the regular British fashion of pressing home a stiff attack, cunningly led that German on a wild-goose chase through the skies, behaving generally in such a manner that Herr Hun firmly believed that his antagonist was scarcely worthy of his mettle; yet, every British bird bagged was one less to annoy the 'brass hats' in the rear of the German lines. Therefore, the German swooped upon Captain Dixon, and showering his bullets all about the machine, fully expected to see the tricolour-marked 'plane go hurtling to the ground. But a far different thing from that happened.

Captain Dixon, with the knowledge that a couple of other British machines were up after the Teuton, had deliberately turned himself into a decoy; and all his strange antics—his fighting and flying away, his apparent helplessness and his evident nervousness, which made the German sure of him—had been most admirable fooling, deliberately designed to lead the enemy on, distract his attention, and allow the two other 'planes to get well above without being seen.

The design succeeded beyond the captain's hopes. The British 'planes, tiny specks in the distance, mounted higher and higher, and through their binoculars the occupants could just see the chase taking place. Up and up, and still up they soared, till they were lost in the void—and never an inkling did the Teuton have of the swift destruction awaiting him.

All his attention was taken up by the foe who was so hopelessly out-matched in every way; never was man so surprised as he when, as though from nowhere, there came two smothering storms of shot which tore through fuselage and planes and—worse than all—struck his engine and petrol tank, so that he went spinning down.

And, as his rival fell. Captain Dixon's machine performed queer antics in the air to celebrate the triumph, in the which there presently joined the two victorious aeroplanes which he had so cunningly assisted.

Second-Lieutenant H. S. Shield, R.F.C., won his Military Cross on September 13th, 1915, by attacking a German Albatross when flying over Bois-de-Biez. He was 10,000 feet up, when his observer. Corporal T. Bennett, sighted the Albatross flying some 3000 feet below. Losing no time, the British machine dived to the attack. As it dropped, the 'Archies' were crashing furiously, and the machine seemed to be slipping through a maze of bursting shells, which fortunately did no damage, so that Lieutenant Shield was able to get into contact with the Albatross, a biplane whose Mercédès engine could drive her along at a terrific pace and whose machine-gun was mounted in such a way that it could be brought into action at almost any angle. "Very conveniently mounted," the official report says of that gun, and it called for considerable skill on the part of Lieutenant Shield to manoeuvre his machine so that Corporal Bennett could attack with the minimum of risk from the stream of bullets which the German gunner was pouring in. The British machine swept down, then circled to the assault. The German sailed on, but the Britishers were relentless, hanging on to the cross-marked tail and splattering their shots upon the body of the Albatross, and trying to hit the engine, which was almost completely covered in.

Not the least part of Lieutenant Shield's work lay in steering his machine so that the Albatross should serve as a protection from the German anti-aircraft guns, and in evading tricks of the Albatross to lure him to positions where the 'Archies' could get him. The Lewis gun chattered away, the bullets 'pinked' all about the Albatross, dotted its wings with holes, and—best of all—struck the machine in a vital part. Of a sudden, Corporal Bennett saw it make a dramatic side-slip, saw its pilot endeavour to right it before that fatal second came when worse should befall; and then, as all the German's efforts failed, the Albatross tilted up its tail, stood on its nose—and dived through 7000 feet, crashing to earth inside the British lines!

Captain Leslie R. Aizlewood (Yorkshire and Lancashire Rifles, attached to R.F.C.) swept along on his aerial duties between the German and British lines, with shell-holed 'No Man's Land' scudding beneath him, the boom of far-off guns trembling in the air and 'woolly bears' breaking into fantastic shapes as the 'Archies' barked angrily. He was on patrol work, which called for eyes everywhere, lest out of the blue depths enemy machines should suddenly swoop and effect his destruction, or endeavour to slip past him and fly over our lines to spot certain things which the High Command desired to keep from the foe.

For a while the captain saw nothing out of the ordinary, heard nothing more ominous than the roar of his engine and the muffled thunder of the opposing artillery, then there abruptly appeared, as it were from nowhere, five machines, heading directly for the British lines. Their appearance was the signal for Captain Aizlewood to pull his 'joy-stick,' manipulate his elevators, and so drive his machine higher than the oncoming aeroplanes, on whose wings were clearly marked the black crosses of the Hun. Up and up he went, while the Germans winged forward and in due course swept under the watchful pilot, whose idea had been to get between the Germans and their lines, and drive them back. With his Lewis gun ready, Captain Aizlewood was waiting for them, and with his engine going all out, he dived at an appalling speed at one of the foes.

Resisting the temptation to fire as he dropped, Captain Aizlewood, in order to make sure of his victim, held his fire until he was within so short a distance as twenty yards; then he let his Lewis gun spit its vicious rain of bullets, sweeping the German machine from tip to tip, plugging holes here and there, snapping contact wires, and damaging the aeroplane so effectually that its pilot lost control. The machine tilted and side-slipped, and then began to nosedive—the beginning of the end of another enemy.

But the tale is not finished. That downward sweep to such close quarters, and the amazing success of the firing, held elements of danger for Captain Aizlewood, who—so much is aerial fighting a matter of seconds—could not flatten out quickly enough to soar triumphantly over the now helpless enemy but went plunging down toward it. A breathless moment indeed! It is easy to imagine the cool-headed captain manipulating the levers of fate and the wires of life and death in the hope of flattening out before the coming of what might be a fatal collision. But it was not to be: the British machine sped through the short space intervening, its wildly revolving propeller caught in the enemy aeroplane, there was a ripping and tearing, a deafening, maddening roar of engines, something went flying into space—it was part of Aizlewood's propeller—and then, the astonished pilot found his machine free from that of his victim, and the latter went on its way to destruction.

It was an unenviable plight in which the British aviator now found himself. His propeller was broken, his machine had received considerable mauling in that terrific midair collision, and somewhere in the blue were four other German airmen who would jump at the chance of tackling what they would consider a lame duck. Captain Aizlewood, his head clear as ever, tested his machine as best he could, found that it was not altogether out of control, although very nearly so, and with the British lines in front of and below him, the airman headed for the ground. It was a descent perilous enough to try the strongest nerves; and yet, with a machine that would not readily answer to touch, and that indeed might at any moment refuse to answer at all and so send him nosediving to death, he swept toward the up- rushing ground—and made a safe landing!

"For conspicuous gallantry and skill," began the official paragraph which announced the award of the Military Cross to the intrepid aviator.

CHAPTER 18

Against Great Odds

The way in which our airmen won the ascendancy of the air was characteristic of the Briton. It mattered not how many hostile machines might be barring the way to an objective, the British machine would drive in among them and break up their formation, and in many cases send some of their number crashing down to the ground. Time and time again the reports of the Flying Services contained short paragraphs stating in cold official language that "Lieutenant A. attacked a flight of ten enemy aeroplanes, completely breaking up their formation." Sometimes there were more than ten! As a rule, that was all the information made public. Nothing of the swift rush to the tune of a roaring engine, nothing of the gathering of the foes in an encircling movement, nothing of the cheating of death by the amazing skill and staggering pluck of the pilot, nothing of the cool-headedness of a man sitting with a machine-gun spitting out its stream of lead—while from all sides the enemy were striving to plug the engine with shot or cut away the ever-moving tail of the machine with the red, white, and blue circles.

Occasionally, however, some interesting details were published—as in the case of Captain W. A. Summers (Highlanders and R.F.C.) and Lieutenant Tudor-Hart (Northumberland Fusiliers and R.F.C), who in the summer of 1916 when on patrol duty somewhere over the troubled front in France, took the offensive against a flight of no fewer than ten German machines. They were coming toward the British lines to spy out the land, and intending no doubt to leave behind them a few mementoes of such a wonderful feat as having braved the crossing of the lines; for those were the days when generally German aviators merely hovered over their own positions, fearing to cross 'No Man's Land.'

Being so superior in numbers to the single battle-plane, which was a fine two-seater with a couple of guns, the German squadron for once held on its way when the Britisher approached with its engine roaring out a challenge to mortal combat. For a while the Germans thought they had the British machine at their mercy, but they were very sadly disillusioned. Captain Summers, who was the pilot of the two-seater, steered his 'plane so skilfully and worked his Lewis gun so effectively, at the same time that Lieutenant Tudor-Hart with an expertness gained in many an aerial 'scrap' manned the second machine-gun, that despite their strength in numbers, the Germans could neither drive off the British machine nor inflict vital damage on it.

It goes without saying that the British machine did not escape punishment—and pretty heavy punishment, too! What else could be expected, in view of the fact that very often it was engaged in a sharp fight against four machines at once, and formed, as it were, the pivot around which the circling enemies turned, the centre to which streams of bullets pelted with hissing anger? Captain Summers, his begoggled eyes missing very little of what his immediate antagonists were doing, or the others were manoeuvring to do, made his machine perform miracles of evolution—darting hither and thither, swooping down upon some luckless German, or swinging at top speed between two enemies and peppering them with his Lewis gun as he went.

Imagine the fierceness of the fight: the narrow escapes from disaster in the great gamble with death in midair! Captain Summers, who knew that only by taking risks could victory be achieved, piloted his machine in such a way that very often it was within fifteen feet of its immediate opponent. For several long drawn-out seconds collision seemed imminent and impossible to avoid, as the wide-spreading 'planes swept close together, then, with a sharp bank Captain Summers circled round the foe while Lieutenant Tudor-Hart sprinkled the nickel bullets over the German. Then, back again the British machine swept to the attack, which was maintained until the observer noticed that another foe was approaching from above.

Such a moment called for instantaneous action; and Captain Summers was equal to the occasion. Even while his observer was emptying a belt of destructive missiles the pilot pushed the 'joy-stick' over to the right; the machine banked at so perilous an angle that it seemed it could never right itself again, recovered, and then went round in a roaring whirl which carried it out of range of the enemy overhead. A tug of the 'joy-stick' once more sent it rising steeply, so that in a few seconds the foe, all unprepared for such a swift and courageous manoeuvre, was being showered with bullets from above. Then the coming of another Hun from the rear distracted the attention of the Britishers and called for yet further evolutions, each more amazing than its predecessors. Once there came an attack from two foes while the Britons were engaged with a third, and as the enemies swept from front and rear it seemed that escape this time was impossible. But the miracle happened: as the Huns approached, their machine-guns spitting angrily, the British battle-plane suddenly dived, leaving the enemies rushing madly toward each other while Captain Summers drove his machine straight for another foe which had been coming up to the attack from below.

In such a way did the hopelessly outnumbered British pilot carry out his self-imposed attack, and so vigorous was the assault that the German formation was smashed and the various machines began a helter-skelter flight to their lines, followed by their redoubtable foe, who chased them many miles over the German positions and only thought of returning home when ammunition had run out.

Then the Britisher merely turned and sailed away, and no Hun machine could stop it, no 'Archie' could bring it down.

CHAPTER 19

Some Anonymous Heroes

The pre-war novelist used to sit down and imagine all manner of wonderful things in the way of aerial fighting, and many queer and amazing exploits were narrated. But truth has proved stranger than even the wildest fiction, as the various stories told in this book will prove. Here is a story which, if it had been told before the war, would have been laughed at as being at least improbable, if not impossible.

Toward the end of 1915, British airmen on reconnaissance work over and behind the German lines in the neighbourhood of Bruges and Nieuport, frequently noticed an enemy motorcar of great speed racing along the roads as if on urgent business. Whenever this particular car appeared, all other traffic gave place to it, so as to enable it to dash along at full speed. That car became a kind of lode-stone to the British aviators, many of whom tried to put it out of action. Time after time they failed; but one day an airman who, like many others, had frequently attacked the car, made up his mind that he would settle accounts with it. Previously, like his comrades, he had used bombs; but it is not easy to bomb a speeding motorcar!

The British aviator does not like to be worsted, and this particular one had decided that the very next time he set eyes on it he would at all risks disable that car.

The day came when, flying at a considerable height in company with another machine, the aviator saw the motorcar tearing along the road in the direction opposite to that in which the British aeroplanes were flying. The pilot suddenly turned his machine from his companion 'plane, and set off in pursuit of the car. His observer, who understood his pilot's ambition, realized what was afoot, and knew that this time bombs were to give place to the machine-gun.

The occupants in the car had seen the target-marked aeroplane in the distance and they were not at all surprised when it turned and gave chase, past experience having told them to expect this. However, as they had over and over again successfully eluded such pursuing craft, they probably smiled as they told themselves that they were in little danger. Their car was speedy, and such a rapidly moving target was not easy to hit with bombs. The chauffeur sat at his wheel and drove the machine along at a terrific pace; while ever and *anon* the officers whom he was driving turned and looked at the closely pursuing aeroplane.

It was drawing nearer, and suddenly to their consternation the Germans realized that this particular machine was adopting tactics utterly different from those tried by aviators in previous attacks. Instead of contenting himself with travelling over the car and dropping bombs, the pilot of the present craft was coming down in a swift steep dive which it was only too evident to the Germans would bring it immediately over their motor, unless they could get more power out of the engine. But the chauffeur had already opened that out, and not another ounce of pressure could be obtained; so that compared with the speed at which the aeroplane was making its descent the motor-car seemed to be standing still.

The startled Germans had but one hope: the aeroplane was making so steep a dive that it seemed impossible for it to escape crashing to the ground.

But the British pilot had his machine under superb control. He had worked out the whole manoeuvre to a nicety, had judged the speed at which he and the car were travelling, while his observer was ready with his machine-gun, and when the throbbing biplane was within a few yards of the pelting motorcar he opened a hot fire at the occupants. So close was the aeroplane that the aviators could see every action of the Germans. The chauffeur was bending over his wheel, one of the officers was crouching as if hoping to escape the stream of bullets, while another, more courageous, was actually standing up, revolver in hand, and firing for all he was worth in an attempt to drive off the attackers. These, however, were not to be driven off.

With revolver bullets boring holes in their planes and singing unmusically about their ears, the Britishers held on to the tail of the fleeing car, the biplane still at an angle which threatened to send it nosediving into the ground. Even the British observer was not feeling at all comfortable during those last few moments in which his pilot kept the tail of the machine up. Though the feat of levelling up the aeroplane seemed impossible, the pilot pulled his 'joy-stick' toward him, the biplane gave a quick convulsive shiver as the elevators felt the changed pressure of the air, the whole machine rocked like a storm-tossed ship, its nose went up, and the next instant the aeroplane was pelting along in safety, leaving—what? A German motorcar lying helpless upon its side!

For, just as the British pilot sent his steed mounting, the chauffeur of the motorcar, badly wounded by the machine-gun fire, lost control, and the car made a dash for the bank at the side of the road. There were shouts of dismay from the German officers as their doomed machine crashed into the bank, pitching them headlong into a ploughed field, and putting the finishing touch to their little misadventure by turning a complete somersault!

It was a very satisfied pair of aviators who flew back to their companion machine and so, as Pepys has it—home.

In this little story we will call the pilot Smithson and the observer Jones, and hope, for the sake of escaping the ire of those who would object, that we have not by any chance hit upon the correct names. Smithson and Jones went up, on a certain day in December 1915, to take photographs of German positions; and in view of the fact that the whole neighbourhood was alive with 'Archibalds' it was a hazardous task that lay before the aviators. Every clump of wood that dotted the countryside had its hidden anti-aircraft gun, and a startling number of fleecy whorls appeared in the sky at the appearance of the British biplane—an F.E., by the way.

However, as aviators live to the accompaniment of such things, Smithson and Jones were not unduly depressed; in fact, their spirits rose as their machine carried them up into more chilly heights. The air seemed to be full of aeroplanes, all of them belonging to the Allies, for the Germans were not so active in the air just then as they had been at various other times. Not that a swift-moving Fokker might not suddenly appear out of the nowhere, swoop down wagging its tail and spraying a leaden hurricane, and make things generally lively.

Nine thousand feet did Smithson and his comrade climb in about an hour, during which time the splendid camera worked by the observer took such photographs as were considered worthwhile. After rising for another 1000 feet, Jones, looking toward the east, saw a thrilling spectacle—a fast monoplane chasing a biplane—and he thought that it might be a British comrade engaged with a German daring enough to approach the British lines. The chase was going on some good distance away, and about 2500 feet below the F.E., but Smithson pointed his machine's nose in that direction and hastened to take part in the little affair, if it were not unfortunately all over by the time he arrived.

As it happened, he arrived in time; and, judging his position to a nicety, Smithson put up his tail till the machine was almost vertical in the air, and nose-dived for about 2000 feet at a rate with which the air speed-indicator could not cope, being designed to register no more than a hundred and sixty miles an hour! It was a hair-raising drop, and Smithson would not have been at all astonished if the F.E. had folded up its wings and dropped . like a stone. Smithson had little time for meditation, for on approaching he realized that the monoplane was German and, owing to its speed, had the advantage of what was unmistakably a British biplane. So well had Smithson worked out things that when his machine was 500 feet from the two combatants the latter were almost directly underneath him, the monoplane threshing out its bullets at the biplane from a range of about fifty yards.

Smithson let his 'plane dive sheer until it was within 200 feet of the Hun, and then began to flatten it out gradually, in order to avoid straining it too much by a sudden jerk, which might have upset all his calculations.

The result of this manoeuvre placed the F.E., when at a distance of about sixty feet off, just above and behind the monoplane; whereupon the Lewis gun began to rattle, and twenty rounds of nickel were slipped into the German. Evidently this was the first inkling Herr Hun had of the F.E.'s presence, and when he realized it he banked sharply and swung round to meet the newcomer, sweeping immediately beneath him and firing as he did so. The tactics of the German made it necessary for the F.E. to bank almost perpendicularly so as to make a complete circle and thus keep an eye upon the monoplane. The German repeatedly made wide, sweeping circles round the F.E., which was executing smaller circles, Jones meanwhile trying vainly to bring his machine-gun to bear. The difficulty with the gun was afterward explained by the gentleman whom we have christened Smithson, who said:

"Owing to the fact that we were doing complete turns in about twice the length of our machine, the centrifugal force was so great that Jones couldn't hold the machine-gun on its mounting; it swung round, and though the whole gun only weighs 28 lb., he could not pull it square."

Naturally, this was a handicap, especially as the German, in his larger circles, was able to bring his gun into action; and things might have assumed a serious aspect if the monoplane had not suddenly decided to hit the unmarked trail for home, probably because he could see in the blue three more British machines pounding toward him. The German made a sudden dive for Mother Earth, and after him went the F.E. with Jones working his gun for all he was worth and spraying the fleeing foe. It was a ticklish moment, for the 'Archies' were having a good deal to say, and the distance from the earth was rapidly decreasing. Smithson was wondering how long the downward chase would last, when suddenly something happened: the monoplane wavered, side-slipped, dived, and then turned a somersault which brought its wheels uppermost—and the Britishers knew that one of those last bullets had gone home, evidently killing the German pilot.

There was a 7000-feet drop before that monoplane, and it made it in a curious, awe-inspiring fashion, the full significance of which only an aviator can realize. Smithson wrote:

> The evolutions which that machine described falling 7000 feet—with no man at the wheel—were extraordinary, viewed from above, first, wheels up; then right way again; a loop, several cart-wheels, a nosedive; more loops, and several turns on to and off its back, sideways, until it was lost to sight almost on the ground.

Thirty-five seconds only did the monoplane take to drop those 7000 feet, and every one of them was filled with the lusty cheering of delighted Tommies, who in a long stretch of four miles of trenches were standing up and waving their hats and shouting themselves hoarse. A number of the cheering soldiers, however, suddenly made a dive for a dugout, because it occurred to them that the falling Hun was heading straight for them. They just managed to scurry in like rabbits, when there was a crash upon the tree trunks forming the roof of the dugout, and the nose of the monoplane buried itself in the bottom of the 'funk-hole,' the impact telescoping the greater part of the machine. The engine caught fire, the dug-out was filled with smoke, and the four men who had rushed to safety there were all slightly wounded.

Smithson looked at his watch, and found that a lot of valuable time which should have been spent in taking photographs had been taken up in fighting, so he set the F.E. climbing again; but before many feet were registered, the engine shirked, and refused to do any more work. This necessitated giving up all hopes of finishing the allotted work; and so the F.E. was turned toward home, where Smithson and Jones, when they arrived, received a rousing tribute, and discovered that the observer of the biplane to the rescue of which they had opportunely raced had been badly wounded.

After devouring a substantial lunch, Smithson and his comrade motored up to the front line, where the machine had fallen—the German front trenches being about a hundred yards away—and there found a few interesting little articles which were carried away as mementoes of an aerial 'scrap' which they knew might possibly have had a different ending.

In the far-off Garden of Eden things happened during the Great War the like of which Father Adam never dreamed of, and not the least impressive of them were the doings of certain airmen, unnamed.

In the early days of war in Mesopotamia, before it was realized that there would be a protracted campaign, our aviators had nowhere to stable their machines, and the result was that constant exposure to rain and fierce sun ruined them; but, as the campaign progressed and the fighting developed into a counterpart, on a small scale, of the warfare of the Western front, aerodromes were established, and a regular system of bombing expeditions was instituted.

The Flying Corps worked in conjunction with cavalry, and the enemy's irregular horse, their raiders, or their companies of thieves, knew to their cost how effective an arm of warfare the Flying Service was. The lurking-places of the raiders were swept by machine-guns from aeroplanes, and even squadrons of Turkish cavalry were chased by the flying men—in very truth a 'flying column,' but in a far different sense from what had previously been understood by the term.

It is on record that a raid on our camel transport was unsuccessful primarily because the airmen had often before struck terror into the hearts of the enemy, by literally raking them with machine-guns.

Flying in Mesopotamia is by no means a pleasure. A newspaper correspondent with our forces, describing prevailing conditions, said:

> In the hot weather, the conditions for flying are very trying. At night and in the early morning the air at 500 feet is far hotter . than on the ground, and it becomes hotter and hotter until you reach 3500 feet. You must go up 6000 feet before you begin to feel cool. The intense heat thins the oil; you can never run

your motor full out or it will get red-hot. You lose 20 h.p. at a temperature of 115 degrees. Long flights are impossible. After 9 a.m. the heat makes conditions most adverse for flying, and there is nothing to be done in the evening. The wood warps and shrinks in the sun. New machines have to be re-rigged when they come out, and the dust chokes the engines. The sand rises in clouds and blows as high as 4000 feet.

During the rainy season mud sometimes put our machines out of action. After a single day's rain at Oran, a 90-h.p. engine and eight men could not move an aeroplane in the driest part of the aerodrome in the driest part of the camp.

Then there are the floods. An aeroplane at Kurna, or Nasiriyeh, between April and July had the same difficulty in finding a dry spot as Noah's dove. And it is much easier to land than to get away. At the beginning of the campaign, when we were operating in country where the tribesmen were in the pay of the Turks, the landing difficulty increased the odds against the aviators.

As an instance showing how the floods affected the aviation, the following story is worth telling. Like so many of the good yarns of the air, the name of the chief character is unknown. It was in July, 1915, and the anonymous airman, who had gone up to Nasiriyeh, was compelled to descend at the earliest moment; but peer as intently as he might, he could see nothing beneath save water. The whole country was under flood—and as the airman was flying a machine not built to do the work of a seaplane, the task was not particularly enchanting, especially as the airman knew that where he must eventually land there were a number of Arabs.

Now, as on one side of the river the Arabs were friendly, and on the other were hostile, a great deal depended upon which side the aviator landed. It called for some skilful manoeuvring to ensure bringing the machine down in the right place, but eventually he succeeded in landing on what he thought was the friendly side. No sooner had he alighted, however, than a number of hostile Arabs appeared, rushing down toward the riverbank, and evidently intent upon bagging the great mechanical bird. After all he had come down on the wrong side! The position was far from a comfortable one for the unfortunate aviator, for he was knee-deep in water and he had only his revolver to defend himself with, but he determined to put up a good fight. He was just about to let fly at the foremost of the thieving crowd, who were now close to the machine, when to his surprise a series of rifle reports rang out and a number of the enemy went tumbling over, while the rest promptly scattered in all directions.

The aviator presently descried a number of friendly Arabs on the other side of the river, and he knew that help was at hand—help which, as it turned out, meant the saving of the derelict machine; for after the 'friendlies' had poured in a goodly amount of fire, they waded out to where the aeroplane was lying and very soon had drawn it out of danger.

Some day[1] we shall have the full story of the work of our airmen in Mesopotamia, and it will contain many thrilling chapters!

---

1. *In the Clouds Above Baghdad* by J. E. Tennant also published by Leonaur.

CHAPTER 20

The Train Bombers

One of the uses of aircraft in war is to disorganize the enemy's lines of communication, a direction in which much good work has been done by British airmen who have bombed transport columns and cut railway lines.

To illustrate the kind of work done the following stories may be told, beginning with the exploit of Second-Lieutenant H. Long (Durham Light Infantry and R.F.C.). Before going on to the recital of this adventure, however, we will first record another incident in which the gallant lieutenant was concerned.

On September 10th, 1915, he sped across the British lines, over 'No Man's Land' and beyond the German trenches, to tackle an enemy observation balloon-shed, the balloon in which, from the British point of view, had on several occasions proved too useful to the German artillery. Lieutenant Long carried a special bomb, weighing one hundred pounds. Although he was fired at very vigorously by the German batteries as he passed, the airman succeeded in arriving well over the shed without being hit, and prepared to drop his bomb. He was flying in circles and taking aim, when an anti-aircraft battery close by the shed made his position so hot that he decided to deal with the guns and leave the original objective for the time being. So, mounting as high as was practicable, consistently with good aim, he darted toward the battery, and, as he passed over it, released his bomb, which fell plumb upon the guns. Exploding with a terrific roar, it reduced the battery to a mass of useless metal, killing some of the gunners and wounding others.

Not a little pleased at his success, the intrepid airman now flew back to his base and loaded up with another huge bomb, with which he returned to settle accounts with the balloon-shed. The Germans were probably far from expecting that the airman would make a second visit. They were engaged in packing up their balloon when the dramatic reappearance of the aviator caused something like consternation. Long lost no time in getting to business: as he swooped over the spot where the men, looking like flies, were tugging at ropes to haul down the captive monster, he let loose his giant bomb, and as he whirred away there came up to him the resonant roar of the explosion. Looking down, he saw that his aim had not been so good as on the previous occasion: the bomb had missed its objective, although only by a very few yards. No little damage was done in the neighbourhood, however, which was some comfort to the plucky lieutenant.

Three days later Lieutenant Long set out on a different adventure. Information had been received that a number of enemy trains were being moved up toward the front, and it was desirable that they should be stopped. The mark presented by a moving train is not as easy as the uninitiated might imagine, any more than two sets of gleaming rails are quite the best targets. In order not to throw away his bombs, Lieutenant Long, when he came within sight of the speeding trains, dropped to an altitude of only 500 feet, at which, naturally, he afforded a fine mark for anti-aircraft guns and even for riflemen. He kept pace with the trains, which, on the appearance of the aerial enemy, had increased their speed; but his bombs missed the quarry and ploughed up the ground alongside the track.

Determined not to be frustrated, the airman flew back to his base for a further supply of bombs, and then, concentrating upon the foremost train, he returned to the attack no fewer than three times, on each occasion flying at a greater height in order to make the best use of his bomb-sight. It was a case of rapid travelling, quick manoeuvring and nice calculation of the relative speed of the train and the aeroplane; a case, too, of taking hazards of being struck by the incessant fire directed at him while over the train, and especially while returning for supplies of bombs. But the lieutenant courageously faced these perils, worked out his plans, and carried them into execution, with the result that after three journeys he had torn up the railway lines in two places, and so for a time at any rate had prevented troops from being transported to where they were sorely needed.

His success encouraged Lieutenant Long to essay a similar feat two days later, when he attacked a crowded train from a height of 500 feet. Although pestered by concentrated rifle-fire, he managed by most careful sighting to tear up many yards of rails.

Then, as though he had not done enough for one day, that very evening, when the ever-watchful observers reported that troop trains were moving twenty-five miles away. Lieutenant Long gallantly volunteered for further duty.

Again winging his flight over the enemy front trenches, he made for the trains, but a terrific rainstorm, the gathering darkness, and the gusty weather were against him this time, and he was unable to reach the trains in time to hold them up. Not to be denied, however, the airman turned his machine and raced toward Peronne Station—a vitally important strategic point.

It was a flight filled with many dramatic moments, for in the raging storm the elements seemed to be combining to destroy the intrepid human who dared to ignore their power. Long held on tenaciously, and presently, as he drew near to Peronne, other enemies joined in the struggle and he found himself faced by a veritable curtain of fire which barred the approach to the station. The roar of the elements was outdone by the crash of exploding shells, and the darkness was brightened by red-glowing stars from whose beauty death might come swiftly at any moment.

So incessant was the fire, so menacing was the ever-changing pattern of the curtain in the sky, that the aviator perforce gave up his self-imposed task, and, sweeping round, steered away from the darkened station. But not to go home; the explosives he carried had not been used, and the intrepid pilot scorned to carry them back with him! So, climbing rapidly to about 1500 feet, he made for a rocket battery, sent his bomb hurtling downward, and heard it explode. Then the sudden cessation of fire from one of the guns of the battery told that the aim had been true; he had put at least one gun out of action, and the evening's danger had been justified, even although he had not succeeded in his first objectives.

On a certain day in the autumn of 1916 a bombing 'flight' of aeroplanes set off to harass the enemy on his lines of communication. Among the British pilots were Captain Eric J. Tyson (General List, R.F.C.) and Lieutenant John R. Philpott (General List, R.F.C). At length, after many miles had been covered, what looked like a big black worm was seen in the distance.

The two British machines darted off toward the crawling thing, for they knew that it was an enemy train, hurrying up either munitions or troops. Captain Tyson reached the spot first, and dived from a tremendous height until he was within about 300 feet of the train.

The droning of his engine had been heard; anti-aircraft guns barked at him, and riflemen sent up a perfect hurricane of bullets. It was a pretty picture for the artist, but a none too pleasant experience for the man sitting in the frail steed of the air. Suddenly, when right over the train, Captain Tyson loosed his bombs, which fell with resounding crashes and effectually stopped the progress of the train, many of the carriages of which were in ruins.

Captain Tyson was in a tight corner, however. In addition to the firing from the ground he had now to face several enemy aeroplanes which came rushing upon the scene and opened fire as he was dodging 'woolly bears' and rifle bullets. Meantime Lieutenant Philpott had come up and found that the train had been wrecked. Apparently there was nothing for him to do there. Not far off, however, lay the railway station—fair mark for any hostile aviator. He sailed right over, dropping his bombs as he went, banked, turned, and made back to where Captain Tyson was engaged with the enemy machines. During the fight the captain had been severely wounded and his engine had been struck by an unlucky shot, so that it would not fire properly, and was a source of annoyance and danger to its pilot. The captain, however, promptly shed his annoyance and forgot the danger in "the stern joy that warriors feel" when they meet their opponents. Ably seconded by Lieutenant Philpott, he fought a good fight—too good for the Germans, who received such a mauling that they very soon scudded to earth.

Meantime the Germans below were endeavouring to start another of their machines. Neither the captain nor the lieutenant were inclined to allow them to effect their purpose, and, as though they read each other's thoughts, they both dived toward the earth, braving a tornado of bursting shrapnel and singing bullets. Feverishly the Germans toiled at their task, hoping against hope to get their machine up before the dare-devil British should come within effective range: and hoping, too, that one of their own guns might plant a shell where it would put an end to the flying of at least one of the machines.

They hoped in vain. With engines roaring—the captain's making weird protestations at being worked at all—the two assailants thundered into range, and gave the Huns a few missiles which scattered them in all directions and dashed their hope of sending up the aeroplane. Then up again, and with the wind whistling merrily through the holed planes, with crashing guns below them and screaming shells behind them, the captain and his comrade took the unmapped trail for home. It is pleasant to add that later they were awarded the Military Cross, an honour which they had certainly earned.

Another officer who won the Military Cross for train-bombing was Lieutenant A. L. Gordon-Kidd (Special List, R.F.C.), who from a height of 7500 feet sighted an enemy ammunition train—good mark, and fair prey to the hawk of the Flying Corps. Down went the gallant pilot in a breathless dive which carried him to within 900 feet of his quarry. Then, at a touch of the pilot's hand, a bomb went whizzing through the air and crashed into the heart of that train-load of explosives. The destructive missile had been well and truly sighted! There was an upward rush of air, the force of which affected the British machine, and made it difficult for the aviator to keep the aeroplane on an even keel. Below, however, was a sight to hold any man enthralled: the bomb had exploded the ammunition, and what was left of the train was blazing furiously.

Another successful attack upon a train was the work of Lieutenant D. A. Colquhoun, R.F.C. This time the train was freighted with horses—probably intended to haul heavy artillery or to serve as draught animals for commissariat wagons. But, whatever their destined use may have been, few of them lived to serve it, for suddenly out of the sky came humming the deadly aeroplane with tricoloured circles on its wings. The engine-driver opened the throttle of his iron steed, the fireman stoked till the sweat rolled off him. All in vain, the dreaded bird of ill-omen swooped like an eagle from its tremendous height, and with such impetus that it seemed it must crash into the racing train. The pilot, however, had his machine well in hand, and when at a height of about 500 feet he released a bomb which fell with devastating effect full upon the unfortunate train. Many of the trucks were instantly destroyed, and the aviator, from his comparatively short distance, saw the bodies of horses flung into the air and far away from the train.

Second-Lieutenant F. S. Moller (General List, R.F.C.) is another hero of the air whose Military Cross was awarded for bombing a train. Together with several other airmen he took part in a raid with the object of harassing enemy communications and effecting as much damage as possible to the 'dumps' containing accumulated stores of ammunition. Each man knew what he was expected to do, and when, in due course, the raiders arrived over the scene of their proposed activities. Lieutenant Moller set to work. Far below he could see a train on the move, heading toward the British lines, and he knew that there was a fair chance of its being well laden.

Through his binoculars, Lieutenant Moller, as he dived to the attack, made out certain things which convinced him that the train was carrying ammunition, and continuing his descent until he was only about 300 yards up, he began to loose his bombs. The angry 'Archies' barked out their protests at the daring aviator, who, however, took little notice of them, and the ammunition train soon felt the destructive power of British explosives. Lieutenant Moller, having noted the success of his attack, now darted in pursuit of three other similarly laden trains, the drivers of which were obviously attempting to put as much space as possible between their freights and the airman. No doubt there was not a man on those trains who did not know that if a bomb from the raider with the tricoloured targets should fall upon the swaying line of cars there would be an explosion from which few, if any, of them would escape.

But a railway train is at a disadvantage as regards speed when compared with an aeroplane, and Lieutenant Moller had no trouble in catching up with his foes; shells burst around him as he flew, and shrapnel clattered upon the body of his machine. Undeterred, he came up with the rearmost train, swooped, sighted, and his bombs fell with a resounding crash. Spending no further time on the crippled train, the airman caught up with first one and then the other train, treating them with similar severity.

It was a very satisfied British airman who now returned to his base, and not even the incessant fire of the anti-aircraft guns which battered his machine spoiled his enjoyment.

Chapter 21

A Champion Aerial Fighter

Four months at the front, and a hundred fights in the air! Such is the bald statement of facts regarding the record of Captain and Flight-Commander Ball, D.S.O., M.C. Add to this the fact that by the time he had completed those first four months on active service Captain Ball was only nineteen years of age, and one has some idea of the kind of men comprising Britain's aerial fighting force.

It is impossible here to relate even a tithe of his many fights, and we must content ourselves with telling one or two of the exploits of this stern-jawed, keen-eyed king of the air.

He was a second-lieutenant (temporary lieutenant) when, on a day in the autumn of 1915, he destroyed an enemy kite-balloon. Now, in order to bring down a kite-balloon one has to be over the enemy's lines and well within range of artillery; and although the weird-looking sausage is a fairly large target, compared, say, with a Fokker, it is no easy task to drop bombs with any degree of accuracy: the bomb has to hit fairly and squarely. When Lieutenant Ball spotted the kite-balloon he instantly made for it, swooping down upon it as an eagle swoops on its prey. When immediately over it, he loosed his first bomb, which went hurtling down to explode harmlessly on the ground. From below, the anti-aircraft guns began to pepper him; but Ball stuck to his task and bombarded that balloon until he had exhausted his bombs, though, to his chagrin, without having done any damage to his objective.

Driving his machine out of the danger zone, the pilot swept back to his aerodrome behind our lines, loaded up with further bombs, and without wasting a moment of time, took the air again and hied him out across country to the far side of the German lines. There was the kite-balloon, still tugging at its ground lines as though taunting him for his failure. Lieutenant Ball repeated his previous tactics, but with this difference: one of the bombs struck home. Immediately the balloon burst into flames, and with a tail of fire roaring behind it, the basket fell rapidly to earth.

The official announcement of the award of the M.C., "for conspicuous skill and gallantry on many occasions," contained, after a brief account of this exploit, the following cold statement:

> He has done great execution among enemy aeroplanes. On one occasion he attacked six in one flight, forced down two and drove the others off. This occurred several miles over the enemy's lines.

How one wishes for an amplification of that little paragraph, with all its details filled in! But the lack in this instance is somewhat atoned for in the official accounts of how Lieutenant Ball earned his D.S.O., and the two bars thereto.

The day on which he won the D.S.O. was a very eventful one for Lieutenant Ball. First he espied seven enemy machines in attacking formation, and made a dive for them, separating one from the others and driving toward it at a terrific rate until he was within some fifteen yards. At such short distance there is little chance of manoeuvring for position, and it is a case of fighting right away. The Britisher set his machine-gun *ta-tat-tatting*, and from the German machine came an answering song of hate. Bullets from the guns plunked into the machines, flipped through planes, snipped wires which twanged to the rush of air; but, although Ball had many a mark to show subsequently, none of the enemy's shots got home vitally, or caused sufficient damage to put his machine out of control. On the other hand, the German got it hot—the spraying bullets from Ball's gun dealt severe punishment to the Teuton and his aeroplane. The Hun machine was suddenly seen to shiver; do what the pilot would he could not get back control of it; and presently it slithered through the air and crashed to earth.

This was quite sufficient for the other half-dozen Germans, who promptly made off!

The air was full of hostile machines that day, and scarcely had the gallant Ball finished the fight just described when five fresh antagonists appeared in sight. Having still a fair supply of ammunition, Ball went gallantly to the attack, adopting similar tactics and concentrating upon the machine nearest him, which he approached at rapid speed until he was within ten yards of it. For a second time that day he was successful; well-aimed shots hit the German's petrol tank and played havoc with the engine, so that the machine went nose-diving to earth with flames issuing forth from its fuselage.

There was little time to exult over his victory, for Lieutenant Ball during his attack on this machine had been subjected to a rapid fire from another enemy, to whom he now turned his undivided attention. Quick as lightning he swung round to the attack, firing his bullets into the German, and giving his foe neither rest nor respite until he had afforded him the full benefit of every cartridge in his possession. Once again, the enemy machine, badly holed and quite out of control, crashed down on the top of a house in a village over which the latter part of the fight had taken place.

Having used up all his ammunition, Lieutenant Ball winged his way to the nearest aerodrome within our lines, took in a supply, and with a cheery wave of the hand was off up into the air again, looking for more enemies—and finding them. What happened later on was a fitting climax to a brilliant series of encounters; for, meeting three enemy machines, he attacked them so vigorously that the Germans, utterly demoralized, scudded for earth and safety: anywhere, to get out of range of this fearless fighter!

The *communiqué* laconically says:

> Then Lieutenant Ball, being short of petrol, came home. His own machine was badly shot about in these fights.

On the day that he won the first bar to his D.S.O. Captain Ball was on escort duty to a squadron of bombing 'planes, and in the course of the flight he espied four German machines in formation, waiting to attack the British raiders. Instead of giving them the opening they wanted, the lieutenant took the initiative, and being at a greater height than the enemy aeroplanes, dived toward them at such a speed that, in order to avoid collision, the Germans had to break up their formation—which was just what Ball wanted. Before his foes could recover position, he was upon the nearest one, spraying the machine with his bullets and causing such havoc that it went tumbling down to bury its nose in the ground, a complete wreck. Captain Ball seems to have been fond of smashing formations of German aeroplanes, for the announcement gazetting this first D.S.O. bar contains an account of another exploit, in which he went boldly to the attack of no fewer than twelve enemy 'planes!

Adopting his usual tactics, he dived and scattered the enemy forces, firing at the nearest one with such good effect that it was put out of control and went spinning over and over to destruction. He had little opportunity for observing his enemy's end, however, for he had scarcely succeeded in sending the first machine to earth before three others were upon him, attacking from different angles. It was a desperately tight corner, in which an instant's loss of self-control, the slightest negligence, meant disaster! Clear-headed and daring, the pilot darted into the attack, first at one foe and then at another, driving one away—probably too scared to come again within range of such a doughty fighter—and putting a second one out of control so that it went earthward to keep its shattered companion company.

Ball now found himself in anything but a fit condition to continue the fight, for his machine had been badly handled by the enemy, and he had emptied his gun of its last cartridge, whereas he knew that the third machine, which was now coming toward him intent on trying conclusions, was probably well supplied with ammunition The British pilot was under no delusions as to what might be about to happen, and told himself that his flying days were probably over, for the German was humming toward him, with his machine-gun fully trained upon the foe. A few more yards and the spraying bullets would be spattering all about him . . . a few more minutes and his machine would perhaps go spinning to destruction. . . .

Ball, with his eyes fixed upon his onrushing foe, did not try to avoid the combat, for—he had his revolver fully loaded! A revolver against a machine-gun spitting death at the rate of hundreds of bullets a minute! It makes one hold one's breath even to think of it!

Fortunately, that Teuton did not know the straits his enemy was in, or no doubt he would have acted far differently from what he did. As he drew near Lieutenant Ball noticed that the German was seized with a nervous shaking. Probably the fierce onslaughts upon his companions had utterly unnerved him. As becomes a warrior, whether he fights on land or sea or in the air, Captain Ball was quick to seize his chance: he opened fire with his revolver and emptied it full in the face of his foe. A grim dramatic moment! Yet not so dramatic as the moment that followed, for the impetus of his swift flight carried the German on a little way, and then—his machine turned over, and went down . . . down!

Very cautiously the victor banked and turned; then, flying very low owing to the fact that his machine had been badly mauled, Captain Ball returned safely home.

Much more might be told of Captain Ball's achievements, for he had a most remarkable record in the air. In the course of his many adventures he had accounted for no fewer than forty-two enemy machines. Then came disaster. Early in May 1917 it was announced that this gallant officer had been missing since the evening of the 7th of that month. He had gone up with ten other airmen, on a flight the purpose of which was not revealed, and the last that was seen of him was when he was a little way over the enemy lines. Then the light failed, and the aviator, hero of so many fights, took his place upon the tragic list of 'missing,' a list which has contained the names of few men more entitled to the admiration of their countrymen.

ALSO FROM LEONAUR
AVAILABLE IN SOFTCOVER OR HARDCOVER WITH DUST JACKET

WINGED WARFARE *by William A. Bishop*—The Experiences of a Canadian 'Ace' of the R.F.C. During the First World War.

THE STORY OF THE LAFAYETTE ESCADRILLE *by George Thenault*—A famous fighter squadron in the First World War by its commander..

R.F.C.H.Q. *by Maurice Baring*—The command & organisation of the British Air Force during the First World War in Europe.

SIXTY SQUADRON R.A.F. *by A. J. L. Scott*—On the Western Front During the First World War.

THE STRUGGLE IN THE AIR *by Charles C. Turner*—The Air War Over Europe During the First World War.

WITH THE FLYING SQUADRON *by H. Rosher*—Letters of a Pilot of the Royal Naval Air Service During the First World War.

OVER THE WEST FRONT *by "Spin" & "Contact"* —Two Accounts of British Pilots During the First World War in Europe, Short Flights With the Cloud Cavalry by "Spin" and Cavalry of the Clouds by "Contact".

SKYFIGHTERS OF FRANCE *by Henry Farré*—An account of the French War in the Air during the First World War.

THE HIGH ACES *by Laurence la Tourette Driggs*—French, American, British, Italian & Belgian pilots of the First World War 1914-18.

PLANE TALES OF THE SKIES *by Wilfred Theodore Blake*—The experiences of pilots over the Western Front during the Great War.

IN THE CLOUDS ABOVE BAGHDAD *by J. E. Tennant*—Recollections of the R. F. C. in Mesopotamia during the First World War against the Turks.

THE SPIDER WEB *by P. I. X. (Theodore Douglas Hallam)*—Royal Navy Air Service Flying Boat Operations During the First World War by a Flight Commander

EAGLES OVER THE TRENCHES *by James R. McConnell & William B. Perry*—Two First Hand Accounts of the American Escadrille at War in the Air During World War 1-Flying For France: With the American Escadrille at Verdun and Our Pilots in the Air

KNIGHTS OF THE AIR *by Bennett A. Molter*—An American Pilot's View of the Aerial War of the French Squadrons During the First World War.

AVAILABLE ONLINE AT **www.leonaur.com**
AND FROM ALL GOOD BOOK STORES

www.ingramcontent.com/pod-product-compliance
Lightning Source LLC
Chambersburg PA
CBHW021003090426
42738CB00007B/629